The
Giving
Crisis

The
Giving
Crisis

Helping Average Givers
Become Everyday
Philanthropists

ANDREW McNAIR

Forefront
BOOKS

Published by Forefront Books.
Library of Congress Control Number: 2022914879

Print ISBN: 978-1-63763-150-8
E-book ISBN: 978-1-63763-151-5

Cover Design by Bruce Gore, Gore Studio, Inc.
Interior Design by Bill Kersey, KerseyGraphics

*To my wife, who has
tirelessly supported me through the writing process.
To Hines McNair and my parents, because I stand
on the shoulders of godly men and women.*

Contents

My Prayer for You

I *don't know your name, I don't know what little or burdensome finan-cial baggage you are bringing into this book, and I don't know the financial fears or desires that you have. I wish I could meet you in person and pray over you and your family. Thankfully, we serve a God who knows you by name and knows everything that you are walking through.*

Please know that I am interceding for you as you grapple with the content of this book. I'm praying that you feel challenged and emboldened in your faith so that you join the next generation of Christians who will deeply impact the world for Christ.

This is my prayer for you:

Dear Father,

I come to you on bent knees to lift up this fellow family member in Christ. I pray that you strengthen this reader and empower them through your Spirit and help them to be rooted and grounded in love and compassion for others. Honor their commitment to becoming better stewards with what you have endowed them in this life. We want to learn how to better manage our finances not for our glory and comfort but for Your Glory to spread among our neighbors and nations. I pray that after reading this book, they are reminded of your provision to them and your history of provision for your people, that you eliminate any fears or ungodly desires that lie within them. I pray that you will help them be rooted in your love and comprehend the depths of your love that surpasses knowledge.

May your grace be with them. In Jesus' name, Amen.

The Giving Crisis

*Before the judgment seat of Christ my service
will be judged not by how much I have done
but how much I could have done.*

~ A.W. TOZER

O ne of my unbelieving finance professors in college once challenged me, saying, "Are you really a Christian if you're as greedy
as everyone else?" What do you think? It's a harsh question but one that
I think is worth asking. I don't believe that being a good Christian will
make you wealthy. I'm not selling a Prosperity Gospel. But there is some
truth to the idea that, if you see your finances like God does, you will
always live from an overflow of gratitude.

Most contemporary Christians, on the other hand, mismanage
their money.

Based on the hundreds of clients I have served at Swan Capital,
and based on the statistics supporting our findings, the probability that

your life and your finances are out of balance is very high, just like other Americans. Christians are not exempt from life's problems, and the Bible never promises that you will find financial success or never experience setbacks. What I want to show you in the pages of this book is how God can transform our finances, the same way He transforms the rest of our lives.

That is, if we let Him.

The way I believe God does this is by challenging us in our giving. Sadly, most Christians right now are failing the test.

As a church we're not tithing much at all.[1] The numbers are telling:

- Some 247 million US citizens identify themselves as Christians, yet only 1.5 million tithe.
- The average weekly giver contributes less than $1,000 a year.
- Of those who attend church, only 5 percent tithe.
- Eighty percent of contributors only give 2 percent of their income.
- Only 1 percent of households making over $75,000 per year contribute at least 10 percent of their income to their church.
- Seventeen percent of American households currently give less than they once did to local churches. For 7 percent of regular churchgoers, the amounts donated dropped by 20 percent.

You might be thinking this is because Americans are struggling right now for a variety of reasons. You're probably even thinking about how tough it's been for *you* financially. Americans are doing better than they've ever done before. We are the richest generation in human history. And yet more prosperity has not made us more generous.

One report indicated that North American churchgoers gave more during the Great Depression (3.3 percent of per capita income in 1933 than they do now.)[2]

In almost every measurement possible—wage growth, disposable income, income to debt ratio, total household income, and unemployment rate—Americans are thriving financially but languishing in generosity. We tithe less than we did during the Great Depression, during which we had almost 50 percent unemployment.

"Are you really a Christian if you're as greedy as everyone else?"

And that has produced a crisis within the church.

The Giving Crisis

The inability—or unwillingness—of Christians to give financially is hurting our churches and our communities as a whole. Maybe you serve on your church's board or on a leadership team. You've been in those financial meetings. You've had to make those tough calls: what programs to cut, what services to prioritize.

When our leaders present what's happening, they call it a "financial crisis." We don't have enough money to sustain our programs. We don't have money for outreach.

We are not in a financial crisis. We are *in a giving* crisis.

Percentage of U.S. Adults who Report Donating 10 Percent or More of Income ("Tithing"), by Generation

	% Millenials	% Gen-Xers	% Boomers	% Elders
To a church	1	2	3	7
To a nonprofit	3	4	5	8
Did not tithe to a church or nonprofit	95	93	92	85

Collectively, we have plenty of funds to go around. If every Christian tithed, faith organizations would have an extra $139 billion each year.[3] The total income of American churchgoers is estimated to be $5 trillion. Imagine if the church actually received 10 percent of Christians' income. That would be $500 billion annually in church revenue. Imagine what we could accomplish for God with that many resources. We can hardly wrap our minds around what the impact would be if God's people were faithful in their giving.

We are in a crisis because we have neglected the heart of the problem: tithing.

Our witness is suffering for it. We speak Christianity with our lips but our financial accounts say differently. One of my pastor friends once said, "Be sure to only quote dead pastors." So here is one from a deceased pastor, Charles Spurgeon:

> I believe that one reason why the church of God at this present time has so little influence over the world is because the world has so much influence over the church.... The more the Church is distinct from the world in her acts and in her maxims, the more true is her testimony for Christ, and the more potent is her witness against sin.[4]

The church is not standing out against the selfishness and greed of the world around it, and that is a problem. The Lord did not leave this open to interpretation. As recorded in 1 John 2:15–17 (NKJV), John said:

> Do not love the world or the things in the world. If anyone loves the world, the love of the Father is not in him. For all that is in the world—the lust of the flesh, the lust of the eyes, and the pride of life—is not of the Father but is of the world. And the

world is passing away, and the lust of it; but he who does the will of God abides forever.

As Christians, we should be little Christs.[5] We should not blend in. The gospel will not always make sense with the wisdom of the world. In fact, we know by Jesus' words that the gospel will be divisive.

Jesus says," I am here to bring a sword, not peace."[6]

Of course, the Gospel is relevant to our modern lives. There is a difference between staying relevant and accommodating to the point of compromise and, ultimately, becoming the same as the world around us. When I see the trends in Christian tithing practices, I worry about compromise. There is no motivation for people to join a church that promises nothing different than what the world offers. On our current path, the church will become more marginalized.

If you were to compare the bank statements and credit card statements between believers and nonbelievers today, you would be hard-pressed to see the difference.

We're not living up to the standard of faithfulness demonstrated by the early church. If you were to compare the bank statements and credit card statements between believers and nonbelievers today, you would be hard-pressed to see the difference. Look deeper than the account balances and into the behaviors surrounding our spending habits and sadly, you wouldn't find much difference with the rest of the world. This should not be and cannot be. We must no longer look, sound, or act like those who are lost—and that can begin with our finances.

Our situation today reminds me of a church described in the book of Revelation, the church of Laodicea.[7] The Laodicean church had one foot in each camp: in the way of the world and in the way of God. They wanted the pleasures of the world and the fruit of righteousness.

Christ gave us a choice: God's way or the way of the world. There is no in-between. We're either hanging on to our possessions or hanging on to Christ. The world has one way of looking at money; God has another.

God and Money

God has a lot to say about personal finances, but most of us are actively avoiding the conversation. It is my experience that, in church, we hardly ever touch the topic of money. Discussing finances is as taboo in the house of God as it is at the dinner table. We can talk about fasting, about sexual purity, and even about politics—but we steer clear of biblical stewardship.

Are we afraid of offending people? Afraid of coming off as greedy for money for our church? Of preaching a gospel that asks too much?

If you're a regular churchgoer, think about the last time you heard your pastor talk about money. Was it months ago? Years? When it happened, how did it feel for you? Did you squirm a little in your seat? Roll your eyes about another sermon on tithing? Maybe even slip out early?

If you're a pastor, how often are you talking with your congregation about money? Is it just the one time of year when the church is behind budget? Is this a teaching topic you're covering on a regular basis, because you know how the financial health of believers is ultimately a heart issue that can affect their spiritual health?

Without consistent preaching and teaching on money, my fear is we will accidentally lead people into a false religion: a religion which is solely a "get-out-of-hell-free" card and not one which actually changes our lives. A religion which bears no fruit.

Some Christians hold the mistaken belief that the Bible is silent on giving. Nothing could be further from the truth. One count tallies

2,350 verses about money.[8] One-fifth of Jesus' parables involve money. According to *Forbes*, money and material possessions is the second most referenced topic in the Bible, appearing more than 800 times.[9] Money—collecting it, giving it, paying the government, and the dangers of money—is quite present in the Bible.

What about tithing, specifically?

Some dismiss tithing as an outdated Levitical law—but is that the case? It's amazing how many people become overnight biblical researchers when defending their current spending habits.

Tithing has a broader foundation than Levitical code. We can trace tithing all the way back to the first book of the Bible: Genesis. In Genesis we encounter the story of Abraham, called by God as the Father of many nations. Abraham's story is the beginning of the story of the people of God, the Jews. Chapter 14 describes his quest to rescue his nephew, Lot, from his captors. When he returns successfully, he gives 10 percent of his spoils to the priest-king Melchizedek. The author of Hebrews, a book in the New Testament, affirms Abraham's tithe.[10]

Later in Genesis, Jacob, grandson of Abraham, vows to give 10 percent of everything to God.[11]

You might be asking, "What about grace?" It's true. We must remember that because of the New Covenant, we Christians are now covered with a layer of grace that wasn't known in the Old Testament. Grace never lowers the bar for living godly lives.

In fact, we learn from the Sermon on the Mount that grace *raises* the bar. The Law was only the beginning. It was a starting point. It set the standard for us to follow. The Law reveals to us our own reluctance to give; it reveals our selfishness. As New Testament Christians, we are challenged to give even more. As we grow in spiritual maturity, the tithe becomes something we feel eager to give, not a check we feel obligated to write. The 10 percent required by Law becomes a baseline for our giving—not the maximum amount.

There is one New Testament passage, in particular, that Christians point to in an effort to release themselves from tithing. Paul writes in 2 Corinthians:

> Each of you should give what you have decided in your heart to give, not reluctantly or under compulsion, for God loves a cheerful giver. And God is able to bless you abundantly, so that in all things at all times, having all that you need, you will abound in every good work (2 Corinthians 9:7–8 NIV).

I have heard pastors use this Scripture to say that tithing is not necessary because Paul didn't require it of the Corinthians. "Tithing is not a command," they say. When Scripture becomes difficult to swallow, we are tempted to soften it.

As much as this passage talks about giving what you can, Paul goes on to teach that we should give abundantly. Our response to God's generosity should be our own generosity. How can we be filled with grace but have no gratitude? How can we give Jesus our eternity but not our earnings? How can we go to church but not give to the church? Paul's admonition to the Corinthians is a challenge to give more, not a permission slip to give less.

The Bible speaks loud and clear on money. We can't ignore it.

Why People Don't Tithe

Beyond excuses about personal finances and priorities—and simply plain procrastination—there are a few common reasons people cite as to why they don't put money in the offering plate (or, more recently, give online). By definition, tithing is giving a tenth to the church, while giving is over and above the 10 percent to ministries and charities. Let's go over some of these common excuses why people don't tithe or give.

"I must take care of my family first."

When Natasha and I started dating, I brought her roses every week. I would come into her work every Friday with half a dozen or so roses. She would smile ear to ear and say, "Andrew, you are my Romeo." I had trouble back then fitting my big head out the door when she called me "Romeo."

One night Natasha came to visit me at my office for the first time. I gave her the office tour, which ended in showing her our lobby. At the front receptionist's desk, she saw a vase full of roses. She asked, "Andrew, what are these for?"

The Bible speaks loud and clear on money. We just ignore it.

"Oh, we give every client that visits with us a rose," I replied. "It's a reminder that it's only money after all, and to smell the roses."

She gave me a squinted, uneasy glare, and that's when I realized I was in trouble. The flowers looked familiar to her. She asked hesitantly, "Are these the roses that you give me every week?"

I responded timidly "Yes, I always give you the ones we have left over at the end of the week. She replied, "Andrew, it's really sweet that you bring me these roses, but these were meant for someone else first. These aren't *my* roses, these are your clients' roses."

That evening I learned a valuable lesson: that order matters. Yes, we should prioritize water, electricity, food, and shelter. Proverbs 3:9–10 says, "Honor the LORD with your possessions, and with the firstfruits of all your increase; so your barns will be filled with plenty, and your vats will overflow with new wine" (NKJV). He doesn't say second fruits or last fruits. He gives us the priority list for our funds. Natasha always wondered why the roses were a little wilted. What does our offering look like to God at the end of the week?

"We give in different ways."

I have met with families who have told me, "Andrew we give to a lot of organizations, but we don't give to a church. We give in different ways other than money. We give our time and other resources."

Those gifts are important. However, that mindset is in opposition with scripture in Malachi where God accuses his people of robbing Him because they neglected to prioritize God's house. God's house is your local church.

"I don't know where the money is going."

If this is your excuse, I'd like to ask, "Do you know exactly where all of your money is going in your personal life?" Many families don't have a budget (let alone a budget committee) they have to answer to. I'll address later in this book why I think traditional budgets are mostly ineffective for individuals and families. For now, my question here is this: have you taken a look at your own financial management practices before critiquing your church?

Most churches have a group of responsible people trying to do the best with the church's finances in service of the gospel. If your church doesn't have this—and if you're already managing your own money well—maybe it's a service you can offer.

Sadly, there will always be churches that get it wrong. There are leaders and pastors who steal and shame the rest of the body of Christ. Before we judge the church, we should attend those budget committees and look in the mirror of our own money-management practices.

"I think my pastor is already overpaid."

I doubt your pastor is living as high on the hog as you think. Many pastors are dual-career staff members and do not have enough support from their church to be a full-time pastor. Some pastors rely on a spouse's income or take a second job.

Is there church leadership in place which publishes the pastor's salary? If not, you don't know what your pastor gets paid and you don't have intimate details of his finances. Before you jump to conclusions, step back and ask if this is merely an elaborate way for you to avoid doing what you know God has called you to do.

More importantly, should your pastor's salary determine whether or not you are obedient to God in your giving practice? It is your responsibility to give. It is the committee's responsibility to determine how the funds are allocated.

Finally, if you're genuinely concerned that your pastor gets paid "too much" (because there are definitely overpaid pastors in our country), be reminded that you do not have to stay at the church where you are currently attending. You can find a smaller, more community-oriented church if that's what you prefer.

"God will provide for the church, so I don't have to."

God will surely provide, and God doesn't need your money. As the psalmist writes, "For every beast of the forest is Mine, And the cattle on a thousand hills."[12] He does not need sacrifice (of animals, of money, of anything else). The purpose of tithing is transformation and witness, not God's need or ability to provide.

Sometimes the most "religious" people are those who resist giving the most. If we are not careful, we will approach Jesus just like the Rich Young Ruler (RYR) did—as someone who lived the letter of the law but did not want to give from his heart.

Jesus' conversation with the RYR sounds a lot like a conversation He had with a group of lawyers, which was recorded in the Gospel of

————————

In this book, I hope to show

you God's way of giving.

As you'll discover,

I had to learn the hard way.

————————

Luke. Both the RYR and the lawyers came to Jesus with the same question: "What shall I do to inherit eternal life?"

Jesus answered with the same reply: "Do you know the commandments and have you followed them?"

Both arrogantly agreed that they knew the commandments and even followed them to a T. They were religious, observant, proud people—and they thought they had aced the test.

But Jesus knew the inquisitors' hearts—and He cared enough not to brush them off or let them go. With the lawyers, He challenged them with the story of the Good Samaritan. With the Rich Young Ruler, He challenged him to give up his possessions. Each had to choose: would they let go of their possessions to help those who were "different" from them?

Like the RYR and the lawyers, we also find ourselves wanting the good life—and an eternal one. Which do you want more?

A Better Way

In this book, I hope to show you God's way of giving. As you will discover, I had to learn the hard way. When you learn God's plan for your giving, you will become more content, more fulfilled, and more joyful. You will also join what I call the Giving Generation—a generation of Christians who are going to systematically minister to those who are suffering, get rid of any greed within the church, and finally answer the Great Commission to reach the unreached people groups in the world. A movement of Christians who get to participate in God's eternal kingdom. A segment of believers who will be remembered as starting a revival of radical generosity within the church.

In order to become part of this movement, we're going to have to go deeper with our finances than we've ever gone before. We're going to have to ask the tough questions. We're going to have to challenge ourselves to take uncomfortable new steps forward.

Do you get more riled up about a college football game than you do about tithing? If so, you're not crazy. You are certainly not alone; you are missing out on the abundant life that God promises, and you are missing out on the contribution to the world that you could be making.

Our life preaches to the world what we prize. If our life only reflects our consumption and our striving for success, we haven't even begun to experience the abundance God has for us. Giving is a living testimony to where we put our faith. Therefore, give not for the glory of others but instead give to reflect God's glory and to shine a light that will encourage other believers to give too.

If we are not careful, Christ will come back, and He will not be welcomed in our churches. Instead, He will find Himself knocking on the door, waiting to be let inside. Christ will see the cross on the door, but He won't be recognized, honored, respected, followed, or heard. Not to mention, He won't recognize *us*.

A revival is necessary. A Giving Crisis can only be remedied by a Giving Generation. I believe we have everything we need to become that generation—to learn the upside-down world of Christ, to become the most generous generation in human history, in addition to being the wealthiest. It won't come without sacrifice.

In the pages of this book, I hope to show you how you can become part of the Giving Generation and how you can inspire those around you to do the same. Imagine what would be possible if we gave from the wealth of what we've been given. You may not have to imagine it much longer. Those who you do life with, lead, and disciple pay attention to how you steward your finances. What better way to disciple than by living out and practicing radical generosity? I know you want this, and I'm confident you can do it—so keep on reading!

CHAPTER 1

The Worry-Free Money Formula

*The measure of a life, after all, is not
its duration, but its donation.*
~ CORRIE TEN BOOM

I wish you could have been there in my room. Picture me—a pretty regular teenager—screaming into my pillow and punching my mattress as hard as I could. I felt like I was completely out of hope, completely missing direction in my life.

I was only nineteen, but I'd already been on a long journey.

For me, it started with a book: *Rich Dad, Poor Dad*. I read it in high school, at a time in my life when I was neither rich nor poor. My dad was a government worker, and we were solidly middle-class. However, my parents valued education, so they enrolled me in a local Christian private school. There I met friends whose parents were wealthy business owners, investors, and entrepreneurs. I was a middle-class kid in an upper-class world, and I felt the difference. *Rich Dad, Poor Dad* gave me the financial wisdom that many "rich kids" hope to receive.

I have to be honest. The book challenged me and absolutely ignited a fire in me to become something my parents didn't have the opportunity to be: rich, young, and powerful.

I learned about investing money. I learned about income-generating assets. I fell in love with the idea that you could make money in your sleep. I was hungry for all the information I could get my hands on, so I asked my parents to teach me more. Feeling ill-equipped to teach me about the financial world when they themselves weren't knowledgeable about it, they decided to schedule a trial internship for me with a financial advisor, who happened to be a lifelong friend of the family.

Looking back on it now, I see that this was a God-ordained meeting. I've met thousands of advisors in my thirty years of life, and none of them have made the impact on my life that my first mentor did. In my opinion, he was one of the smartest people in finance: he knew his stuff.

There I was, a fourteen-year-young boy working for zero dollars an hour. The financial advisor had me doing everything from taking out trash to filling out financial models. I was building financial plans—and nothing had ever been as exciting.

Soon enough, I realized that most of the people coming into the office weren't millionaires. In fact, even when they were, they were frugal, disciplined people who lived on a budget. As for me, I was thirsty for more. I didn't want to be like them. I wanted to be *rich*.

So I picked up another job—one that actually paid.

When I told my friends I couldn't hang out on the weekends anymore, they protested, "You have to join us this weekend! There's going to be the best house party!"

"No," I told them, "I can't go out. I have to start saving for retirement."

My friends laughed, "What do you mean, save money for retirement? You're fourteen years old!"

They couldn't shake my determination. I couldn't even drive, so I had my parents drop me off for my shifts as I waited tables at Denny's. I saved everything I could. I tracked everything. I became Dave Ramsey on steroids. I budgeted down to the last penny and saved everything possible. I worked every weekend, every holiday, and any spare moment I had. In less than two years, I had saved $62,000. I was a sixteen-year-old swimming in cash.

Still it wasn't enough for me. So I made new goals: I wanted to retire at forty. That's when I turned to the stock market.

It was 2008, the beginning of a great recession. For most people, it was a terrible time in the market. I watched as people lost their life savings. I watched 401(k)s get cut in half, and yet I also knew the most basic principle of investing: buy low, sell high. So for *me*, this was a great time in the market; the perfect time to invest. With diversified investments, my savings grew quickly. Soon I had $147,000.

I found myself addicted to earning money. If you've ever been addicted to anything—from Netflix to Instagram to drugs—you can predict the end of this story before I even tell you. Things started to spin out of control. I began to believe I had the Midas touch: anything I touched would turn gold.

But I was in deep trouble and didn't yet know it. I was nineteen years old with over a hundred grand saved, but I was never satisfied. The bar kept rising higher, and the life I was working for still felt far away.

And it was about to get even farther away.

The Hard Worker's High

These three adjectives described the life I was after: rich, young, and powerful. I wanted to make enough money so that while I was still young, I could enjoy it. I wanted to retire early. I wanted to be seen as an influential person, sought after for my connections and influence. I wanted to make it to the top. I wanted "the good life." I wanted to make waves.

I set my sights high, and I enjoyed the challenge. I liked getting up early. I even liked staying late at work. I didn't mind missing the weekends out with my friends. Too many movies and books portray "the hustle" as painful. I never felt that way. Instead, I experienced what I call the "hard worker's high." Like a runner's high, it's a new well of energy, a second wind with a sense of euphoria. Many other successful people agree: when you put your head down and start making progress, the work itself becomes its own reward.

I took "workaholic" to the next level. In college, I was still working a full-time job in the finance industry while also waiting tables. I finished my degree in three years—diploma in hand, a six-figure income, and a kind of overachiever's PTSD to prove it.

By all accounts, I had met my goals: I was already a millionaire. I was only 23. I felt powerful because I spoke in front of large crowds and had built a business with the title "CEO" on my business card. I had made it; I was rich, young, and powerful.

I thought I had everything I wanted.

Why did I still feel empty?

If you're anything like I was (and still am), you're ambitious, and you dream big. You want good things for yourself. You want a better life for your family. You want to feel alive—rested and energized. You're doing well, but you look forward to a day when you can slow down and enjoy your hard work. Ideally, you'd like to retire early, and pass the good life on to your kids and grandkids. In the end, you'd like to have made some kind of contribution to the world. You want a life you can be proud of.

If that's you, then perhaps you'll relate when I confess that never once did I feel satisfied with my net worth. Despite my money, I always felt like something was missing. There was always something in me pushing for more. Whenever I crossed a threshold, the finish line jumped farther ahead. While people around me applauded my accomplishments, the silent voice in my head said, "Oh, you think you succeeded? You could do so much better. You could be so much bigger."

I competed with the worst opponent: myself. My own voice egged me on, saying, "You think a million dollars a year is impressive? You can make $10 million a year." That voice, however, is never satisfied. It never rests or feels fulfilled. It says, "You were never *that* successful. Not really."

When you live with this voice, you're always looking for what's next. Though your experience says otherwise, you still believe the next level will make you happy. You work as hard as you can. Except your highs are never as high as your lows are low. You're going full speed toward a finish line that keeps outpacing you.

Are your thoughts on what God might have in store for you or what God might have to say about your life? You left those considerations way back at the first mile marker.

My point is this: too many of us—Christians especially—work and hustle until one day we realize we're on a treadmill. As much as we crank up the pace, we're still running in place. What are we honestly striving for?

Maybe you read this story and think I sound like an immature boy (it's okay, I was). My guess is that there's some part of you that also resonates with my approach to life and money in those days. You have a drive you can't explain. You want to achieve something remarkable. You push yourself and work hard to provide for yourself and your family. At the end of the day, whatever you accomplish or earn never feels like quite enough. You're always looking for more.

Deep down, perhaps you suspect the truth: even *as you meet your goals*, the fulfillment and purpose you're looking for is getting farther and farther away. Despite your experience, it's really hard to let go of the idea that money will bring you what you are after. When you take a step back and look at our larger culture, it's not hard to see why.

The Lie of the American Dream

The American dream is the promise of "life, liberty, and the pursuit of happiness." On a surface level, that seems to be working for us. As a country, we've never been more blessed. Sure, it's easy to point out the negatives of our society, but look at what is going well for us: We are wealthier than ever. We can travel where we want and can communicate with people across the world. We have more discretionary time than ever. Even a decade ago, who had time to stream as much content as we do today?

We are also more depressed and more anxious than ever. Researchers and behavioral scientists have been on the search for answers to the unsettling rise in depression and anxiety. It is a timely question: How can Americans who live in one of the most prosperous countries, within a Golden Age of history, still be so predictably unhappy? Swiss psychiatrist and psychoanalyst Carl Gustav Jung wrote, "About a third of my cases are suffering from no clinically definable neurosis, but from the senselessness and emptiness of their lives. This can be defined as the general neurosis of our times."[13]

There could not be a more perfect assessment of our current crisis in America. Could it be possible that anxiety and depression are a result of a constant pursuit of more?

A quick assessment of how we spend our time and money will tell us that we're obsessed with "more." The pursuit of happiness comes, culture tells us, through buying and having and doing.

Think about our heroes: our celebrities make headlines based on their spending. We're impressed when someone buys out an entire shoe

ould work harder. Maybe that's why you haven't made it."
urselves for being "behind" and we fall into depression.
s while Jesus whispers in the background to *sell everything we*
w Him (see Luke 18:22). How have we gotten this so wrong?
ninute about the myriad of ways we're suffering for it. "More"
ave us empty. Andrew Carnegie, despite his failure, was right:

ssing of wealth is one of the worst species of idolatry.
more debasing than the worship of money. Whatever I
n I must push inordinately therefore should I be careful
se the life which will be the most elevating in character.
inue much longer overwhelmed by business cares and
ost of my thoughts wholly upon the way to make more
in the shortest time, must degrade me beyond hope of
ent recovery.[14]

the richest men in the world discovered—through his
t money makes a terrible god.

own, I believe that most people want to achieve not only
ves but for the world around them. Of course you want
th, and power—but more than that, like Andrew Carnegie,
ltimately want *significance*. It's just that somewhere along the
sucked into this rat race of success and we can't turn off the
ays, "You're not enough. This is not enough!" What starts as
an Dream turns into an American nightmare—one where
ing success and never arriving. Pursuing happiness and never
A purposeless chase that leaves you empty.
at's the solution? A 180-degree turn. When it comes to our
ow we acquire it, what we do with it, and our relationship to

store or throws an extravagant wedding. The American Dream sells us overconsumption and idolizes those who have endless resources that never seem to run out; that lifestyle, even if attained, does not bring satisfaction. In addition, what the media never reports is that the new-car smell wears off. People who think that they'll find purpose when they buy their dream home or when they finally have their private jet will realize later that they were wrong. It doesn't fulfill them. You simply don't hear those stories. Wealth can make us extremely unhappy if we don't have a God-sized plan for what to do with it.

The True *Gospel of Wealth*

Take, for example, an iconic man famous for achieving the American Dream:

Andrew Carnegie. His life is the original rags-to-riches tale. Carnegie was born into poverty. Early in his life, he watched his father go bankrupt, as new technology made his work obsolete. Witnessing his father beg for money put a real chip into his shoulder. His family left Scotland looking for a land of opportunity.

Having to end his education after only five years of schooling, Carnegie went to work as a young man. His wit and work ethic helped him rise through the ranks of the telegraph company he worked for and again in the railroad company he was employed by.

As he became an investor and, ultimately, the owner of a steel manufacturing enterprise, Carnegie never planned to work forever. He planned to clock out at age thirty-five. When he died, his list of goals were found tucked away, which read: "I will spend the first half of this life accumulating money and I will spend the last half of this life giving it all away." In fact, Carnegie made the following promise to himself: "By this . . . I can so arrange all my business as to secure at least 50,000 per

—————

Wealth can make us

extremely unhappy if we

don't have a God-sized

plan for what to do with it.

—————

annum. Beyond this never earn—mak[ ]
spend the surplus each year for benev[ ]

Despite Carnegie's good intentio[ ]
Why? Because the same drive to do [ ]
me had overcome him. His company [ ]
of overworking his people (364 days [ ]
wages, giving their jobs away to inc[ ]
workers with machines that did th[ ]
Andrew Carnegie a robber baron for [ ]
workers.

So much for income-capping and b[ ]
here? Can you relate?

In the entrepreneurial world, Car[ ]
accomplished. Even when Carnegie's [ ]
country's entire gross domestic produ[ ]

At age seventy, he sold Bethleh[ ]
richest men in history.

Carnegie *did* finally go on to do[ ]
While it's wonderful that Carnegie wa[ ]
true happiness and freedom, the quest[ ]
what takes us) so long? As we read i[ ]
on philanthropy, it took him *seventy*[ ]
about money. He spent most of his li[ ]
cial trauma he experienced in childho[ ]
life trying to cover his sins with benev[ ]

His story is typical. The numbers [ ]
same for millions. This is not hardly co[ ]
any church today and you'll find pews [ ]
and lack joy. Comparison eats away at [ ]
asks, "Do you have any possessions? A[ ]

Well, yo[ ]
We puni[ ]

All o[ ]
own and [ ]
Think fo[ ]
will alway[ ]

The [ ]
No i[ ]
enga[ ]
to ch[ ]
To c[ ]
with [ ]
mon[ ]
perm[ ]

One [ ]
wealth—[ ]

Deep[ ]
for them[ ]
wealth, y[ ]
you and [ ]
way we g[ ]
voice tha[ ]
the Ame[ ]
you're ch[ ]
catching [ ]

So w[ ]
money—[ ]

it—most of us need to turn everything we know on its head. Jesus calls this repentance. I call it the day I found myself screaming into my pillow.

Don't Waste Your Life

I was nineteen when I lost everything. It was dumb. I started doubling up on certain investments. I tried to predict what would do well. Eventually, I made the mistake of putting it all—my entire $147,000—on one company.

That company went bankrupt, and just like that, everything was gone. It was the worst day of my life because I felt bankrupt too. I had confused my self-worth with my net worth. Yet it was the best thing that ever happened to me.

I remember screaming, crying into my pillow. I spent hours in my room. I was devastated, but I wasn't mad about the money. I was upset because of the time I had lost: all those weekends and holidays I had worked, all the time I had skipped spending time with friends and family. I could never relive those high school years.

I vowed to myself, "If I ever do this again, I will do it differently." I knew that something was wrong with the way I had lived my life up until that point, but it still took me a while to figure out *what*.

Worry Free Money Formula

$$FW^2 \text{ (Financial Worries)} = \frac{\text{You in charge of your \$}}{\text{Time (how long it takes to figure out you're not in charge)}}$$

$$FC^2 \text{ (Financial Confidence)} = \frac{\text{God in charge of your \$}}{\text{Time + God's will}}$$

I kept finding success. I made a million. I made another million. The wealth seemed to pour in, and I congratulated myself for all of my hard work. In the end, I wasted more than a decade of my life obsessing about money before I realized the secret to a more meaningful, fulfilled life—one that doesn't exclude the possibility of great wealth. I wish I would have known and trusted in the Worry Free Money Formula before it was too late. If your finances have ever felt out of control, impossible to juggle, or overwhelmingly stressful, the Worry-Free Money Formula is the equation you need. Giving money always will. That's the Worry-Free Money Formula.

It was the worst day of my life because I felt bankrupt too. I had confused my self-worth with my net worth. Yet it was the best thing that ever happened to me.

My prayer is that you don't waste a decade of your life like I did and like Andrew Carnegie did. It's not worth it. The rat race of getting up early and working late, of sacrificing in every other area of your life until you reach some finish line that isn't even there, will always leave you empty.

Psalm 73 reads, "But as for me, my feet had almost stumbled; my steps had nearly slipped. For I was envious of the arrogant when I saw the prosperity of the wicked" (Psalm 73: 2–3 NRSV). We have to remember that "more" is a black hole we cannot fill. Once we reach that "success" by our previous definition, we find that our happiness plateaus and the emptiness reappears.

Perhaps by earthly standards, you have everything, yet deep inside, you might feel like I did for much of my twenties: you are spiritually bankrupt. Isn't it incredible how we can be surrounded by earthly treasures and yet have no treasures stored up in heaven? The American store or throws an extravagant wedding. The American Dream sells us overconsumption and idolizes those who have endless resources that never seem to run out; that lifestyle, even if attained, does not bring satisfaction. In addition, what the media never reports is that the new-car smell wears off. People who think that they'll find purpose when they buy their dream home or when they finally have their private jet will realize later that they were wrong. It doesn't fulfill them. You simply don't hear those stories. Wealth can make us extremely unhappy if we don't have a God-sized plan for what to do with it.

The True *Gospel of Wealth*

Take, for example, an iconic man famous for achieving the American Dream:

Andrew Carnegie. His life is the original rags-to-riches tale. Carnegie was born into poverty. Early in his life, he watched his father go bankrupt, as new technology made his work obsolete. Witnessing his father beg for money put a real chip into his shoulder. His family left Scotland looking for a land of opportunity.

Having to end his education after only five years of schooling, Carnegie went to work as a young man. His wit and work ethic helped him rise through the ranks of the telegraph company he worked for and again in the railroad company he was employed by.

As he became an investor and, ultimately, the owner of a steel manufacturing enterprise, Carnegie never planned to work forever. He planned to clock out at age thirty-five. When he died, his list of goals were found tucked away, which read: "I will spend the first half of this life accumulating money and I will spend the last half of this life giving it all away." In fact, Carnegie made the following promise to himself: "By this . . . I can so arrange all my business as to secure at least 50,000 per

----

Wealth can make us

extremely unhappy if we

don't have a God-sized

plan for what to do with it.

----

annum. Beyond this never earn—make no effort to increase fortune but spend the surplus each year for benevolent purposes."

Despite Carnegie's good intentions, he didn't retire at thirty-five. Why? Because the same drive to do more and be more that overcame me had overcome him. His company and right-hand man made a habit of overworking his people (364 days of the year), shrinking his workers' wages, giving their jobs away to incoming immigrants, and replacing workers with machines that did their jobs for them. People called Andrew Carnegie a robber baron for the ways he used and abused his workers.

So much for income-capping and benevolent giving. What happened here? Can you relate?

In the entrepreneurial world, Carnegie gets praised often for all he accomplished. Even when Carnegie's net worth was 2 percent of the country's entire gross domestic product, he didn't stop.

At age seventy, he sold Bethlehem Steel and became one of the richest men in history.

Carnegie *did* finally go on to donate all of his wealth to charities. While it's wonderful that Carnegie was able to finally realize the path to true happiness and freedom, the question remains: What took him (and what takes us) so long? As we read in *The Gospel of Wealth*, his book on philanthropy, it took him *seventy years* to finally realize the truth about money. He spent most of his life overcompensating for the financial trauma he experienced in childhood. He spent the final part of his life trying to cover his sins with benevolence.

His story is typical. The numbers are different, but the story is the same for millions. This is not hardly confined to the 1 percent. Walk into any church today and you'll find pews filled with people who are restless and lack joy. Comparison eats away at us. That familiar voice returns. It asks, "Do you have any possessions? Are you powerful or famous? No?

Well, you should work harder. Maybe that's why you haven't made it." We punish ourselves for being "behind" and we fall into depression.

All of this while Jesus whispers in the background to *sell everything we own* and follow Him (see Luke 18:22). How have we gotten this so wrong? Think for a minute about the myriad of ways we're suffering for it. "More" will always leave us empty. Andrew Carnegie, despite his failure, was right:

> The amassing of wealth is one of the worst species of idolatry. No idol more debasing than the worship of money. Whatever I engage in I must push inordinately therefore should I be careful to choose the life which will be the most elevating in character. To continue much longer overwhelmed by business cares and with most of my thoughts wholly upon the way to make more money in the shortest time, must degrade me beyond hope of permanent recovery.[14]

One of the richest men in the world discovered—through his *wealth*—that money makes a terrible god.

Deep down, I believe that most people want to achieve not only for themselves but for the world around them. Of course you want wealth, youth, and power—but more than that, like Andrew Carnegie, you and I ultimately want *significance*. It's just that somewhere along the way we got sucked into this rat race of success and we can't turn off the voice that says, "You're not enough. This is not enough!" What starts as the American Dream turns into an American nightmare—one where you're chasing success and never arriving. Pursuing happiness and never catching it. A purposeless chase that leaves you empty.

So what's the solution? A 180-degree turn. When it comes to our money—how we acquire it, what we do with it, and our relationship to

Dream is selling us lies. Having money will never satisfy. Giving money always will.

Today I own a successful investment company which has helped hundreds of individuals and families take great care of themselves and their families—not through the relentless pursuit of more, but by helping them give away more of their income, year after year. In many cases, my clients are able to *give away* the majority of what they earn. What I watch happen for each one of these clients might surprise you, or it might not. Their joy grows the more they give away.

There's a common misconception around money that I find many Christians hold. I hear this misconception all the time. Clients will try to quote a verse from the Bible and say something like, "Money is the root of all evil." Did you know the Bible doesn't say that? What the Bible *says* is that the *love* of money is the root of all evil (1 Timothy 6:10).

For me, making money has come fairly easily but making *meaning* out of my money has not. It's taken me over a decade to learn that money doesn't become satisfying until we learn to give it away. If there's one thing I want to leave behind when I'm gone, this is it.

Every day it's my mission to revive the sound financial principles of a poor carpenter's son, born 2,000 years ago, by the name of Jesus of Nazareth. All this time later, Jesus still has the longest lasting money-back guarantee on what it means to be rich, young, and powerful. His way is countercultural—but it's the only one that works.

You'd be shocked how many Christians think they understand giving, but ultimately they're not much different than I was at nineteen years old. They're in a relentless pursuit of something they can only have when they learn to give it all away.

As you learn the biblical view of wealth, you'll experience a deeper peace around your finances and a stronger sense of joy and meaning. In order to get those things, you're going to need an open mind. So ask yourself this question: In what ways has modern culture shaped my ideas about money? Is money making me happy or unhappy?

We're working with high stakes here. Mark 8:36–37 (NKJV) says, "For what will it profit a man if he gains the whole world, and loses his own soul? Or what will a man give in exchange for his soul?" This is a question you will have to answer for yourself.

As for me? I would give my millions.

Chapter 1: Reader's Guide

Biblical Text to Study Revelation 3:14–22

Discussion	• How does having limited margin in our finances limit our spiritual walk with Christ? • Why is it easy to see ourselves as *not* rich? • In what ways are you chasing the American Dream, and how is this keeping you from God's purposes? • Are there areas of your life where you are feeling empty? • What do you think about the author's belief that anxiety and depression come from an unwillingness to give?
Framework	**The Worry-Free Money Formula** Go back to the Worry-Free Money Formula and ask yourself: Who or what equation or method is driving your decisions around money?
Memorization - Commit this verse to memory over the next week.	**Revelation 3:19,** *As many as I love, I rebuke and chasten. Therefore be zealous and repent* (NKJV).

Group Leader Questions	• What can we learn to avoid from the ways of the Laodiceans? • Are there areas in your life where you are fighting against God's correction (We all tend to hate correction and despise discipline.) • What kind of financial worries have you had that you have taken to God? • Is there anything in your life that is good but distracts you from God? • Have you stolen God's glory lately?
Action Item	Pray about giving every day for the next 30 days. Ask God to open your heart to determine not how much you should be giving but also how much you need to keep. Send your prayer to: prayer@richyoungpowerful.com
Prayer	Lord, I pray that our country wakes up to its blindness and spiritual deficit and feels the weight of its shame and nakedness in front of you. Lord, please continue to knock on the hearts of the lost and plead louder to the souls that are cold and against you. Help our lives and words be testimonies of love and light to those around us who are blind, lead us to repentance when we go astray, and help us to find the contentment that can only be found with you.

CHAPTER 2

The Surprising Key
to a Rich Life

I have tried to keep things in my hands and lost them all,
but what I have given into God's hands I still possess.
~ MARTIN LUTHER

Jesus came to us as a poor man, but He brushed shoulders with rich and powerful people. One such encounter is recorded in the Gospels, where Jesus meets a man we have already noted, a man famous today as the Rich Young Ruler.

The RYR approached Jesus and asked a big question: "Good Teacher, what must I do to inherit eternal life?" (Mark 10:17) The man was looking for what matters, what lasts.

Jesus responded by recounting commandments, to which the RYR replied defensively. He insisted he had done all the right things, at least according to his own estimation. He told Jesus, "All these I have kept. What do I still lack?" (Matthew 19:20).

THE PLAY-DOH TEST

Do you remember the first time you played with Play-Doh? Can you still feel the texture in your hand? I can remember as a kid watching everyone roll their dough into a ball and the smart kids making objects out of it. Meanwhile, there I was, squishing it in my hand, marveled by it coming through between my fingers. The harder I squeezed, the more deformed the Play-Doh became.

If we are not careful, this is exactly what will happen if we cling to our possessions too tightly.

We can mold anything out of our lives. Yet instead of choosing to mold our inalienable talents and gifts into something kingdom-focused, we choose to cling to our physical possessions so tightly that our lives become deformed. Our Father in heaven sees how we cling to our toys and beckons us to open our hands and share with others. Just as a father chastens and disciplines his children when they do not comply, God too correctly disciplines us—until we pry one finger at a time off of the life that has been gifted to us.

What are you squeezing so tightly today? Whatever it is, let me challenge you to let go of it.

———————

It's not our posses-

sions *themselves* that

keep us from God. It's our

attachment to our posses-

sions. It's our unwillingness

to be generous with what we

already have been given.

———————

The Gospel of Mark reports that Jesus looked at him and loved him. Then Jesus gave him the *key* to meaning and purpose, to a life that lasts forever (eternal life). He said, "You lack one thing: go, sell all that you have and give to the poor, and you will have treasure in heaven; and come, follow me" (Mark 10:21). Jesus gave him an invitation to let go of what held him back.

And how did the ruler respond? "Disheartened by the saying, he went away sorrowful, for he had great possessions" (Mark 10:22).

You've probably heard this story at least a dozen times. It gets recounted often among Christians. But the reason I'm sharing it with you is that I think this story just as often gets misinterpreted. I've heard this story told as a way to say that it's our possessions getting in the way of the kingdom of God. I don't think this interpretation quite captures the essence of what Jesus is saying.

It's not our possessions *themselves* that keep us from God. It's our *attachment* to our possessions. It's our unwillingness to be generous with what we have already been given.

We are the Rich Young Ruler in the story. We must be a people that recognizes our spiritual poverty, our need for not more good things but for *God* things. As Jesus said in His Sermon on the Mount, "Blessed are the poor in spirit, for theirs is the kingdom of heaven" (Matthew 5:3). As Christians, we should be fighting to give our wealth away.

What It Takes to Be Rich

When my grandmother passed away, my grandfather found himself living alone for the first time in sixty-seven years. As I was the youngest in the family, my mother asked me if I would consider moving in with my ninety-two-year-old grandfather—and I quickly agreed. I saw it as my good deed to help out the family. In retrospect, I thought my grandfather needed me, but I found out that I needed him. I see now that my grandfather was the one performing the good deed.

I didn't know how badly I needed mentoring—or what seeds my grandfather would plant in my life.

Living with my grandfather was like stepping inside a time capsule. He had an old shag carpet and a flower-patterned couch in the living room, a yellow toilet with a matching shower, and a dining room right out of the *Saturday Evening Post*. His front yard was adorned with a perfectly trimmed lawn and fragrant azaleas, and, in the garage, he had a Toyota Camry with only 2,000 miles on it.

Talking with him was like opening a history book, except he didn't merely know history; he had *lived* it.

His stories of the Great Depression made quite an impression on me. He helped me understand the gravity of a 25 percent–plus unemployment rate—how men and women had plenty of work ethic to go around, but no work to do. He told me about the sullen faces standing in line for food and the various ways the scrappy survived—even by hunting squirrels. As he described it, the weight of uncertainty and financial desperation back then was like a thick fog over our country.

During the Depression, my grandfather's family owned a small grocery store in Pensacola, Florida. Even an essential business like that one could never quite rest easy. He recounted how the people of the town couldn't pay his father (my great-grandfather), who ran the store, for groceries.

My grandfather closed his eyes as he said, "My father couldn't stand for people going hungry while the store shelves were full."

Back then, it was common practice to keep a tab at the grocery store. My great-grandfather let the tabs grow long, knowing the people would probably never pay him back for groceries. My grandfather's smile reflected, *Not a good business decision, but a good faith decision*. He knew my great-grandfather was doing the Lord's work.

As if that weren't enough, the story continued.

A decade later, long after my great-grandfather had sold the store and retired, a neatly dressed man rang the bell at their home. The stranger addressed my great-grandfather, saying, "You may not recall me, but I frequented your store in Pensacola during the thirties. You gave my young family the food we needed to survive when we couldn't pay you. You never asked for the money, but I haven't forgotten the debt that I owe you, so here in this envelope is everything I owe you and a little bit more."

This is the kind of example that my great-grandfather set for his family and for his community.

My grandfather took that lesson of generosity to heart and, by the time he was in his nineties and telling me this story, I could see what kind of life he had lived: a modest one, marked by generosity. He gave to his country, serving in the US Navy through three wars. Even with a spouse, three kids, and only one income, he gave 10 percent of his income to his church throughout his entire life. He also took a reduction in his pension to protect his wife. He retired early to be active in his church and spend time visiting people in nursing homes, some younger than himself. When he lost his wife of sixty-seven years, he continued to trust God's plan for his life.

What was crazy to me is that as I was striving to be young, rich, and powerful, my grandfather had what I genuinely wanted—all without striving for it. He had something that most people don't ever attain: contentment and purpose. He didn't chase after "more." He didn't have a lot of money or things, but he felt he had enough—and enough to share. He lived his life for God, his country, for his family, and for his community. He had energy that carried him into his nineties. His life was *rich* with relationships, purpose, and joy.

In observing my grandfather's life, I'm convinced his happiness, fulfillment, and impact had something to do with the lesson his own father taught him during the Great Depression about the importance of giving. Money, to him, was only a tool: a tool to help people and to invest in eternal riches.

My grandfather was not the only one out there who found peace and fulfillment through a life of radical generosity. He was part of what would become known as the Greatest Generation: Americans born between 1900 and the 1920s, a generation marked by honor and self-lessness. You probably know some of these people. My guess is that they might be some of the most generous people you know. If you ask me, the Greatest Generation was *great* because they were a giving genera-tion. They were onto something—something that gave them riches later generations haven't tasted, despite being wealthier than ever before.

At the time, I didn't understand what my grandfather was teaching me. I would still have a few more years of making money solely for myself before I had the epiphany that making and spending money would never get me what I was looking for.

But maybe—just maybe—*something else* could.

The Something Else That Changes Everything >>

Christians have been preaching generosity for centuries. Jesus spoke about giving. He taught a crowd, saying, "Give, and it will be given to you: good measure, pressed down, shaken together, running over will be put into your bosom. For with the measure you use, it will be measured back to you" (Luke 6:38 NKJV). Jesus instructed His twelve disciples, saying, "Heal the sick, cleanse lepers, raise the dead, cast out demons. Freely you have received, freely give" (Matthew 10:8 NKJV).

While speaking to church leaders in Ephesus, Paul said, "In all things I have shown you that by working hard in this way we must help the weak and remember the words of the Lord Jesus, how he Himself said, 'It is more blessed to give than to receive'" (Acts 20:35). His relay of Jesus' words has become a well-known passage.

The modern-day takeaway is this: giving is not only a blessing to others, but also a blessing to *us*. We don't learn to be generous because it's a "good thing to do for other people." We learn to be generous because without generosity in our lives, we become anxious, depressed, self-loathing, and searching for meaning. Maybe Jesus teaches us so directly about generosity not only because He wants us to be good witnesses, but because he's teaching us to nourish our own hearts and souls.

Giving is not only a blessing to others, but also a blessing to *us*.

The Old Testament teaches generosity as well. The book of Deuteronomy teaches, "If among you, one of your brothers should become poor, in any of your towns within your land that the LORD your God is giving you, you shall not harden your heart or shut your hand against your poor brother, but you shall open your hand to him and lend him sufficient for his need, whatever it may be" (Deuteronomy 15:7–8). The text goes on to specify that the people of God should give freely and not begrudgingly (Deuteronomy 15:9).

The books of the Bible known as Wisdom Literature outline two kinds of people: righteous and wicked. Psalm 37:21 says, "The wicked borrows but does not pay back, but the righteous is generous and gives." Proverbs 21:26 reads, "All day long the wicked covet, but the righteous give and do not hold back" (NRSV). Another translation of the same verse reads: "All day long he craves and craves, but the righteous gives and does not hold back" (ESV).

All day long we crave, all day we hear the voice of "more, more, more." The voice of craving—of always desiring more—is an age-old problem.

The age-old solution? Giving.

When we are generous with our money, our time, and our skills, we create joy, fulfillment, and purpose for ourselves. This idea is backed by science. There are plenty of studies out there linking giving with a sense of joy and satisfaction.

But we don't need science to know that this is experientially true. Think of the last time you gave someone a gift. Think of how it made you feel to be able to surprise them and to show them that you care. Think of Christmas. The magic of Christmas doesn't come in receiving gifts but in the opportunity to give them. Think of any time you've made, or even bought, a meal to share with someone. Think of all of the things you provide for your family: these are gifts, and you are happy to share them. More than that, being able to provide these things is a strong motivation in your life. It gets you up in the morning. It keeps you working hard.

We act like buying more will give us the fulfillment we want in life. As it turns out, we can *create* that feeling by giving to people and causes that we are invested in.

Giving It Away

Learning how to give was not a lesson I figured out on my own. Scripture convicted me. At age twenty, I had already been giving financial advice for a year. I found that I hit my stride working with older military veterans, offering them investment advice. I was seeing a lot of success. It soon became clear that I should start my own business, so I did: I built a total wealth management company with a CPA and an attorney and began serving high-net-worth families. The year I graduated from college, I was making six figures—more than my dad had ever made. I was astounded by my own success, bringing in more than my dad ever had in his thirty-seven years working for the federal government.

I was living the book *Rich Dad, Poor Dad*.

The upward spiral continued, but as I described earlier, something was missing. Even though I was making more and more, I felt emptier and emptier. I would regularly forget what I was striving for. Why was I making all this money, anyway? This stress didn't confine itself to my finances. I started wondering why I was going to work, why I was going about my day, and why I was on this planet at all. That nineteen-year-old screaming into his pillow was still living inside me.

I had everything, and yet I still asked God, "What do I lack?"

That's when God spoke to me through His Word, in a parable about another rich man. You may think you know this story, but I hope you read it here with a fresh new perspective.

There was a rich man who was clothed in purple and fine linen and who feasted sumptuously every day. And at his gate was laid a poor man named Lazarus, covered with sores, who desired to be fed with what fell from the rich man's table. Moreover, even the dogs came and licked his sores. The poor man died and was carried by the angels to Abraham's side. The rich man also died and was buried, and in Hades, being in torment, he lifted up his eyes and saw Abraham far off and Lazarus at his side. And he called out, "Father Abraham, have mercy on me, and send Lazarus to dip the end of his finger in water and cool my tongue, for I am in anguish in this flame." But Abraham said, "Child, remember that you in your lifetime received your good things, and Lazarus in like manner bad things; but now he is comforted here, and you are in anguish. And besides all this, between us and you a great chasm has been fixed, in order that those who would pass from here to you may not be able, and none may cross from there to us." And he said, "Then I beg you, father, to send him to my father's house—for I have five brothers—so that he may warn them, lest they also come into this place of torment." But Abraham said, "They have Moses and the Prophets; let them hear them." And he said, "No, father Abraham, but if someone goes to them from the dead, they will repent." He said to him, "If they do not hear Moses and the Prophets, neither will they be convinced if someone should rise from the dead" (Luke 16:19–31).

For me, reading this passage in my early twenties was like getting slapped in the face. I had lived the first economic chapter of my life for my personal benefit only, and it had proven exactly as unfulfilling as you would expect.

Yet I still had time. I could turn over a new leaf. My story was not over, like that of this rich man in hell.

I thought to myself, *What if I don't spend my money? What if I start giving it all away?* It sounded pretty crazy, but I like crazy ideas. I started with houses: I bought as many houses as I could. I renovated them, then gave them away to charity. I liked the way I felt when I gave, like I was finally doing something worthwhile.

So I kept giving. I decided I would cap my income—create an artificial ceiling on my income where I would pretend like I never made more than that amount, no matter how much I would continue to make. My income from then on was fixed.

What's crazy is that, when I made that decision, I only continued to make even more profit. Like I mentioned, I made my first million by twenty-three, way faster than I could have anticipated. Shortly after that, I was making a million each year. I had enough money not to work another day if I didn't want to.

Today, I am able to live on only 10 percent of my income. The rest I contribute to a fund, from which I pool to give to charities, churches, and other organizations.

Keep in mind that I started by working at Denny's, tracking every dollar I earned. Now I'm able to give hundreds of thousands of dollars away. I can tell you with 100 percent certainty that giving away money has been more meaningful than making it.

As much as I've tried to give, I've found that you cannot outgive God.

I can't even begin to count the blessings that have come from finally turning my attention to giving. I've been able to watch veteran families move into renovated homes. I've been able to watch kids with disabilities honored as special guests. I've been able to see houses and schools built. I've helped missionaries spread the Word overseas as well as seen the success of local missions trips. All of that has given me joy and a sense of purpose that I never felt by buying a new car or property for myself.

Do I ever miss the high of spending on myself? Sure, as a recovered addict remembers the high of a drug. I was addicted to success and materialism and trying to become the youngest, richest, and top of the heap in my industry. However, in the same split second, I am thankful to remember the agonizing emptiness that my sin left. Giving without expecting anything back has transformed my life from the inside out.

As much as I've tried to give, I've found that you cannot outgive God. Trust me, I have tried, but it doesn't work. The blessings keep on coming back—not always materially, but always spiritually.

Best of all, I've started to experience some of that fulfillment that I saw in my 93-year-old grandfather. I feel at peace knowing that every part of my life—even my finances—are serving a purpose. What I actually needed to do all along was always within my ability: turn around and give.

You and I do not have to walk away disheartened, as the Rich Young Ruler did. We have the opportunity to create fulfillment in our lives through giving.

Chapter 2: Reader's Guide

Biblical Text to Study Mark 10:17–31

Discussion
- Do you see yourself as rich?
- What do you think about the Rich Young Ruler? Do you think people still walk away sorrowful today?
- What are some items in your life or your home that you admit need to go?
- Are finances an area that you struggle to let the Lord into?
- Was Jesus asking the RYR to sell all of his possessions or to trade them in for something better?

Framework

The Play-Doh Test
If you are able, get your hands on some real Play-Doh and try this test for yourself. Keep it close by so you can remind yourself regularly what happens if you cling to your blessings too tightly.

Memorization

Mark 10:27 *But Jesus looked at them and said, 'With men it is impossible, but not with God; for with God all things are possible"* (NKJV).

Group Leader Questions
- What strikes you about what the RYR said to Jesus?
- The RYR approached Jesus as a teacher instead of Lord. How do we still do this today?
- In the past and even today, wealth is thought to represent God's favor. What do you think?
- From the passage, how can we see God's compassion for the RYR?

- Peter asked Jesus, "Then who can be saved?" Are our hearts more focused on the least we have to give up to follow Christ? What is the most we can give and follow Christ?

Action Item	Practice letting go of something that feels like it has a hold on you. What materially (like Play-Doh) has stuck to you? Think of something you already have that someone else might need, and see if you can meet their need without thinking twice about it.
Prayer	God, teach me to see myself as rich and to be generous with everything I have. Where I find myself in resistance, show me the multitude of ways that you have given to me so that I will be quick to let go. May I discover the great joy and blessing that you have built into the act of giving. Amen.

CHAPTER 3

Religion Is Reasonable, Christianity Is Costly

A religion that gives nothing, costs nothing,
and suffers nothing, is worth nothing.
~ **MARTIN LUTHER**

My dream is to witness a generosity revival in the church, to see a generation discard infatuation with material goods, power, and youth. I long to see a giving generation that lives for worthy causes, which invests in impactful ministries, and sees their entire lives, including finances, as part of the mission of God.

Instead, the number one question I get asked as a financial advisor today is: When is the next financial crisis coming? We need to be less worried about the next recession or depression. We need a focus on the Giving Crisis that is already here. I hope to see us step up and stand out as a community dedicated to helping the poor, protecting the powerless, and spreading the news of God's love. I want us to be known for our generosity.

What's getting in our way is not what you might expect. What's getting in our way is *religion*. Let me explain.

Religion is the outward representation of our faith. It is the traditions and rules. It is what society/culture deem as Christianity: going to church regularly, socializing with the "right" people, staying away from certain activities. Religion is a series of motions to go through.

Religion is full of rituals that are easy to practice and rehearse. After a few years of learning the expected rules, anyone can master it. It doesn't require much to go to church, say a prayer, and throw loose change in the offering. After going through these common rituals, many walk out feeling better about themselves.

In the New Testament, the Pharisees, the teachers of Jewish Law, appear again and again as symbols of obedience to the letter of the law without heart transformation. In the Gospel of Luke, Jesus says,

> "Now you Pharisees cleanse the outside of the cup and of the dish, but inside you are full of greed and wickedness. You fools! Did not he who made the outside make the inside also? But give as alms those things that are within, and behold, everything is clean for you. But woe to you Pharisees! For you tithe mint and rue and every herb, and neglect justice and the love of God. These you ought to have done, without neglecting the others" (Luke 11:39–42).

Notice that the Pharisees tithe: they give to God. They follow all the laws about what is clean and unclean. But they fail to do what really matters: protect justice and spread the love of God.

Just as religion hindered some in the first century, it hinders people today. Religion asks *only* what is *reasonable*. The claim it makes on your bank account and your calendar is a small one. It doesn't prevent you from being successful in the world. The Pharisees were highly respected. They had political power. According to their society's standards, they were doing well.

Maybe we, like the Rich Young Ruler and like the Pharisees, can say, "I have kept the commands." We're following the religious rulebook. Tasks like "Sunday church" and "tithing" are items we check off our to-do lists, and we do them faithfully because we believe in them. Tithing and biblical stewardship can never become a checkbox of spiritual piety. If we are giving online, we must continue to pray over our tithes, that they be used for the spreading of the gospel. If they occasionally feel like chores, it's not because we don't see the value in them. We're just a little distracted, a little restless, and eager to get on with making our lives meaningful.

We are rushing past the exact place that could finally provide some purpose—and actually make a difference in the world. That's because religion doesn't ask for much, but it doesn't give very much either. Putting on a religious front will not keep you from being caught in the same meaningless chase for more that the rest of our culture is trapped in. Religion will not provide you a meaningful and purposeful life, and it will certainly not help the church stand out or make a lasting difference in the world.

There is a big difference between what *religion* asks of us and what the *gospel* actually preaches. To follow all the rules is quite different from having a changed heart.

A Crossless Christianity

When we read about the poor carpenter from Galilee, we see anything but reasonable. What He preached flew in the face of many cultural norms: He told His followers to let their dead bury themselves (Matthew 8:22), to strive to be holy and perfect (Matthew 5:48), to love those who hated them (Matthew 5:43), to believe He was the only way to heaven (John 14:6), to die to themselves and to follow Him (Matthew 16:24), and even to drink His blood (John 6:53).

Jesus is as unreasonable about money. Jesus said you have to make a choice between God or money (Matthew 6:24). He asked the Rich Young Ruler to sell everything he owned. We tend to want Christianity without the cross. We don't mind Jesus going to the cross, but we don't want to go to the cross with our possessions. Unfortunately, it doesn't work that way. The gospel is costly. It costs even what is most precious to us.

We want Christianity without the cross. We don't mind Jesus going to the cross, but we don't want to go to the cross with our possessions.

One of the best illustrations on this topic is known as the anointing at Bethany. In the Gospel of Mark, a woman approaches Jesus as He is at the house of a man identified as Simon the Leper. She breaks an alabaster flask of ointment and pours the expensive oil over His head.

Some in the crowd reflect the voice of reason, saying, "Why was the ointment wasted like that? For this ointment could have been sold for more than three hundred denarii and given to the poor" (Mark 14:4–5). Jesus sides with the woman, defending her. The alabaster flask was expensive—and is now broken. The flask was filled with pure nard, an oil imported from India. In those days, the oil in that jar was worth one year of pay. This woman understood that she was in the presence of a king, someone to be anointed. She did not bring Jesus something inexpensive, but something of great worth.

True Christianity doesn't only require our "extras"—but everything, even our best. As the Gospel of Matthew says, "For the gate is narrow and the way is hard that leads to life, and those who find it are few" (Matthew 7:14). True Christianity requires more because it is so much more valuable; justice and love for one's neighbor—*that* is worth sacrificing for.

Are we ready to become that kind of sacrificial community?

The Original Giving Generation

If we want to be the Giving Generation, we can look to the church described in Acts, which modeled this for us. They shared everything, all of their possessions, so that no one was in need. These early believers weren't concerned with spending or accumulating. Instead, they were converting earthly currency into kingdom currency.

In the twenty-first century, this is extremely hard to grasp. Can you imagine how radical this would be in a modern, capitalistic society? You might think it sounds like communism or socialism, however these early church practices would be radical even for a communist society. The acknowledgment that God knows better than the state? That would be radical. What would this look like today? I think it would be characterized by three things.

1. **Unity**

    A giving church is a united church. Jesus unites people from different political, geographic, and racial backgrounds. In God's church, people from all walks of life become one family. Generosity and unity go hand in hand. As we invest our money in our communities, we will start to help each other in other ways, too.

    If we are ever going to become a giving generation, we have to unite under one flag: Christianity.

2. Giving to the church

We can't buy people citizenship in heaven (or buy ourselves a ticket there), but money will practically help kingdom efforts. When we give to church ministries, we help people spiritually and practically. Not only will more people hear about the gospel, but God's love will be shown through physical provision. If we as a body would all begin to surrender just 10 percent of our finances to the church, imagine how many in need we could provide with aid.

3. Giving over and above 10 percent

Jesus called us to a completely different life—an abundant one. The letter of the law—tithing 10 percent—is a great place to start. But the money or the percentage were never the main point. Think of the parable of the widow's mite: she gave so much less, in money, into the offering box than the rich people did (Mark 12:41–44). The Gospel of Mark says what she gave was worth a penny.

Yet which gift did Jesus value more? The widow's gift was a *great sacrifice*. She was willing to give much more than a tenth—she gave everything she had to live on. Her heart was in total surrender. The result? A witness that actually reflects God's love.

What if we viewed what we have as not "mine" and "yours" but "ours"? How would that change our lives? How would it improve our witness? If we want spiritual revival to take place in our country, then we must not only preach about revival, pray about revival, and worship hoping for revival—we must give sacrificially toward a revival. In my opinion, the best witness we can have is our generosity. This was, perhaps, one of the keys as to why the first-century Christian movement spread so rapidly.

We must live radically in order to be different from those around us. Think of what could happen today if hardworking Christian families decided to no longer idolize the American dream and instead replaced it with a dream of seeing the gospel preached and enacted. A revolutionary gospel will beckon a response. People will have to ask, "Why?" because giving away money and possessions—instead of gathering more—is so shocking.

At the end of the day, if the poor and needy are not cared for, the church has failed. And we *are* failing. The services that once made a way for orphans, widows, and the poor to survive are presently underfunded.

Yet so many of us are unmoved and fail to see a connection between our generosity and these problems. I have witnessed professing Christians complain about taxes and, nearly in the same breath, condemn giving to the church. In essence, they were saying, "I don't want the government to help the needy, nor do I want to support the church to help the needy." How far we are from a Christlike perspective.

Lord, convict our hearts if we have been guilty of this attitude toward the government and the church.

The truth is, as Christians, we are not giving nearly as much as we could. Instead, we play by religion's rules. We're lulled into thinking that living by the letter of the law will save us.

I shared these statistics in the introduction. But in case you skipped over them, or have quickly forgotten them, they bear repeating.

1. Some 247 million US citizens identify as Christian, but only 1.5 million of them tithe.
2. The average weekly giver gives less than $1,000 a year.
3. Of those who make it to church, only 5 percent tithe.
4. Eighty percent of tithers only give 2 percent of their income.
5. Only 1 percent of households making over $75,000 contribute with tithing amounts of at least 10 percent of their income.

6. Seventeen percent of American households currently give less than they used to in local-church donations. For 7 percent of regular churchgoers, the amounts donated dropped by 20 percent.

To help you get your brain around the contrast of the modern-day "church" and how Jesus saw the church, read this passage from the book of Acts:

> Now the multitude of those who believed were of one heart and one soul; neither did anyone say that any of the things he possessed was his own, but they had all things in common. And with great power the apostles gave witness to the resurrection of the Lord Jesus. And great grace was upon them all. Nor was there anyone among them who lacked; for all who were possessors of lands or houses sold them, and brought the proceeds of the things that were sold, and laid them at the apostles' feet; and they distributed to each as anyone had need (4:32–35 NKJV).

This was the church in the first century. No one claimed that their possessions were their own. One heart. One soul that cared for the saints overseas and was brokenhearted for the unreached people groups of the world. There is nothing new age here. There are no new truths. This was literally the earliest Christian church, before we had centuries to get confused about Jesus' teaching and get it all wrong.

Imitating the early church begins with a dedication to fellowship but ends with examining our finances and especially our giving. Is the way we spend our money reflective of what we believe about the Great Commission and spreading the Gospel?

Here are the facts. As Americans we have never been wealthier. We are one of the wealthiest civilizations in history, in almost every measurement possible: wage growth, disposable income, income vs. debt, total household income, and unemployment rate. Yet we tithe less than we did during the Great Depression, during which we had over 25 percent unemployment. I am convinced that the reason unbelievers are less drawn to the gospel or less likely to attend a church than ever before isn't because they don't want to believe in God. It's because they see such a minuscule contrast between the so-called Christian believer and those who don't believe at all.

The way to close this gap is not only a revival of the church; it begins with one individual at a time who is willing to abandon the safety of religion for the provocativeness of the gospel. Individuals who are willing to go above and beyond the letter of the law when it comes to giving. Individuals, like you, who are ready to live as the early church did.

We are the Giving Generation.

What It Takes to Make a Difference

Jesus' call demands our all. New believers understand this. I was eleven when I found salvation. The Sunday after I was saved, I remember sitting in the pew, on fire for God and having all kinds of radical thoughts. I wanted to get rid of my material things immediately. I wanted to book the next flight to a remote part of the world—true, at eleven I was too young to book a flight myself—to evangelize to people who had never heard the name of Jesus. I wanted to seek out the marginalized in my city and provide help. When I started voicing these ideas to my new brothers and sisters in Christ, I came up against resistance.

Well-meaning religious people responded with, "Slow down! Just relax."

_____

Is the way we spend our money

reflective of what we believe

about the Great Commission

and spreading the Gospel?

_____

Maybe you've experienced something similar. Maybe people have told you that you need to learn more before you go out trying to have gospel conversations, or that you should pray before making any radical changes. Over time, you found yourself lulled into the comfort and rhythm of going to church and, frankly, not doing much more. You'd like to, but volunteering and donating always seem to fall to the bottom of your priority list.

That was religion talking. Religion is moderate. Religion keeps people from radical action. Religion keeps you in a comfortable, culturally

The Ultimate Financial Goal for Life, by Generation

	% all Christians	% Millenials	% Gen-Xers	% Boomers	% Elders
1. Provide for my family	22	31	18	18	13
2. Support the lifestyle I want	15	14	17	13	7
3. Meet my obligations and needs	13	8	15	15	16
4. Be content	11	8	11	15	14
5. Give charitably	11	8	11	15	18
6. Serve God with my money	10	10	9	11	19
7. Establish a financial legacy	7	7	8	6	6
8. Be debt-free	6	6	5	6	4
9. Show my talent / hard work	2	4	1	1	-
10. Other	2	1	2	2	4

THE SAVINGS AND SPENDING PYRAMID

When I was growing up, the food pyramid gave me a visual picture to understand *why* it wasn't so wise to eat 100 percent junk food. I understood by the simple graphic that moderation was the key to living in balance. I want to do something similar for you with this pyramid.

Financial gurus will tell you to save everything you can and live on a shoestring budget now so you can live like a king someday in the future. I don't believe in that—and it is not biblical, either. Living in balance and enjoying every season is essential to a happy life.

Other financial pundits will tell you that you need to budget and watch every penny you spend. When I hear that, it reminds me of the media's weekly hot new diet. It may sound great, but it is simply not sustainable for most

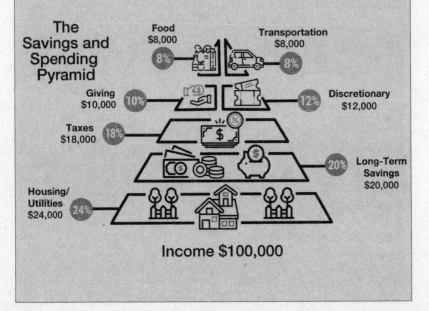

The Savings and Spending Pyramid

Food $8,000 — 8%
Transportation $8,000 — 8%
Giving $10,000 — 10%
Discretionary $12,000 — 12%
Taxes $18,000 — 18%
Long-Term Savings $20,000 — 20%
Housing/Utilities $24,000 — 24%

Income $100,000

people. Your willpower will not be able to stick it out for the long term.

Instead, consider what a healthy savings and spending pyramid looks like. I believe you don't necessarily have to budget—if you prioritize the right things. *Here is my version of the savings and spending pyramid.*

10 percent—Giving

I don't recommend giving only 10 percent, but I do recommend giving the *first* 10 percent. Jesus calls this your firstfruits. My personal belief is that depression and suicide are on the rise not because people are living in tough economic times. I believe people are depressed because they are living for themselves. We were not created to be big enough nor an important enough cause to live strictly for ourselves. Instead, through investing your life and yourself into your community, charitable organizations, and faith, you can find purpose.

Now, that is something to live for.

20 percent—Long-Term Savings

This is what we call the investment trapdoor. Investing long-term does not mean delayed spending. It means saving for your retirement via a Roth IRA and/or 401(k) or other retirement savings vehicle. I believe that you should save 20 percent of your income, if possible, to help you and your family maximize retirement accounts and receive the highest match on your 401(k), where available. Remember, you need to have a healthy emergency savings fund of six months' income before investing long-term above your 401(k) match.

18 percent—Taxes

Now, this number is obviously unique to everyone, but in my experience, it is a figure that many can attain through proper planning. The government is a great inventor of ways to tax its citizens. We must be willing and able to pay those taxes, including property taxes, income taxes, and state taxes. We need to ensure we have allocated enough of our earnings to pay all of those various taxes. We should strive to be a happy taxpayer, one that is concerned enough to participate. What do many people do? I see many complaining, but they don't get involved. If you're unhappy about taxes and where they are going, get involved: vote, volunteer, and talk to your elected officials about their approach to tax policies.

24 percent—Housing/Utilities

Be careful about the house you choose. Be even more careful if you are helping your children buy a home or thinking about helping them with a down payment. One key mistake I see many families make is deciding to move into a too-expensive neighborhood. That's because, in my experience, certain neighborhoods have certain expectations. They expect you to drive a certain car, ride a fancy lawn mower, dress your kids to a certain standard, and attend certain schools. We call it magnetic spending, because some people buy nice things to avoid having friends and neighbors judge them for not living up to their preconceived picture of them.

Your house can cost you more than you think!

8 percent—Food

My eyes have enlarged at seeing families' grocery and dining out bills. America is eating its future away. Food is essential, but I have heard every excuse in the book for not cutting back on food spending. Families have told me that they eat healthy. I politely keep it to myself that my family eats nearly no white starches, consumes a heavy fruit/vegetable ratio, and purchases lean, high-quality meats. The issue for most families is not that healthy foods cost more; it is that most families buy convenience.

8 percent—Transportation

You don't want to neglect your retirement savings because you have luxury cars as depreciating assets. If someone looks down on you for what you drive, you may need new passengers in your life.

12 percent—Discretionary

Entertainment, education, clothing—we need to understand what discretionary spending is. The only four things I believe are basic financial human rights that we all should have are shelter, water, food, and electricity. Always keep in perspective that everything else is optional. Netflix, mobile phones, and even the internet in 2023 are not basic human rights. The local library has free internet if you need it.

I believe that families who follow this savings and spending pyramid or one similar to it can live a more financially balanced life. If you don't live in moderation, it comes at a cost; that cost will be your financial future—*and your giving.* Furthermore, as a parent and grandparent, it is important not only to teach the savings pyramid, but to model it for your loved ones. They often watch your actions rather than listen to your words.

approved Christian life. Religion keeps your finances in relatively the same place: no major sacrifices. You can still spend your leisure time and discretionary income as you'd like. You can still increase your standard of living each year.

As John Piper asked in *Don't Waste Your Life*, "If you could just have a good job, a good wife or husband, a couple of good kids, a nice car, long weekends, a few good friends, a fun retirement, a quick and easy death, and no hell . . . would you be satisfied?"[15] I worry that too many modern-day Christians *would*. But would you?

Or do you want to do something more with your life?

The devil has convinced countless religious people that following Christ doesn't cost you anything. The devil is happy to see you pursue a counterfeit Christianity, a religious charade that doesn't cost you anything but only misleads everyone around you. The devil wants to see millions turn away from Jesus, settling for an empty religion that consists of saying a simple prayer, deciding to walk down an aisle, instead of having a real conversion.

In a similar way, we must not simply tithe in obedience without love. If we are not careful, we will be clean on the outside—looking like "good Christians" who go to church and give—but our hearts will not be right. We will not care for the poor. Instead, we will be greedy.

This is not the Christian life at all. As Christians, we are settling for a religious version of a secular life. I call it practical atheism: when a person confesses Christianity with their lips but does not make any changes to their life.

This is a difficult message to hear. But I want to be honest with you about where I see the church of today heading because I believe we have the opportunity to come together and change that direction. It will be difficult, but, little by little, we can become the generation of givers that the world needs today. Imagine if we started small with our Starbucks habit. (Oops, I am in trouble now!) Here is a practical example: What if you gave up merely one day a week of ritually visiting your local coffee shop and instead enjoyed your coffee at home? Now, you take those new savings to give to one ministry that you feel strongly about, such as Operation Christmas Child Shoeboxes with Samaritan's Purse. In one year's time, your small sacrifice now has accumulated to $750, which could pay the cost of shipping for nearly one hundred children to receive a Christmas present *and* the good news of the gospel. Plus, you increased your annual giving by over 1 percent annually ($14.40 × 52 weeks = $750 / $56,000 average American's salary). These shoeboxes brought such big smiles to the children that their faces began to hurt, and better yet, they received the greatest news that anyone could ever hear. Imagine: one skipped coffee that gives fleeting joy, refunded for an offering that will make an eternal difference.

Chapter 3: Reader's Guide

Biblical Text to Study: Acts 4:32–37

Discussion

- What can we learn from the first-century church?
- How can we apply the Acts passage to our lives?
- What does your current giving look like? What would you like for it to look like?
- Are you living like Christ, or have you settled for simple religion?
- In what ways might God be calling you to something bigger?
- Did you find anything in the savings and spending pyramid that you disagree with?

Framework

The Savings and Spending Pyramid
Go back to the Savings and Spending Pyramid and ask yourself how your own spending reflects the pyramid that I suggest. What can you learn about your own money habits from this exercise? What might need to change? Visit RichYoungPowerful.com/spendingpryamid to download the fillable Savings and Spending Pyramid Diagram to calculate it based on your actual income.

Memorization

Acts 4:32 *Now the multitude of those who believed were of one heart and one soul; neither did anyone say that any of the things he possessed was his own, but they had all things in common* (NKJV).

Group Leader Questions	• What can we learn from the first-century church? • Do you agree that God supplies our needs but not all of our wants?
Group Leader Questions	• Are there other believers in the congregation that need your help? • Can our group sponsor a missionary family? Can we go as a group to minister to the lost and reach them ourselves? • Why can we talk about prayer life, sex, testimony, and other private things in a small group, yet money is hard to talk about?
Action Item	**Check your checking and check your calendar.** If you want to know who or what you actually worship, pay attention to where you spend not only your money but your time. **Make a list of the top ten places where you spend your time.** Maybe it's things like school, work, and home. Maybe there are also some line items like Netflix or video games. As you compile your list of how you spend your time, ask yourself: Who am I trying to please? **Now, scan through your bank account and make a list of your top ten categories of spending.** You have housing, transportation, etc. Then you likely have things like entertainment, clothes, coffee, eating out, and perhaps even alcohol. What about giving? As you look at your list of how you spend your money, ask yourself: Who am I trying to please?

Prayer   God, help us dream beyond our own understanding of what might be possible for our lives
and trust that you will lead us to something
bigger and better if we trust you. Give us the
courage to surrender to the call you have
for us. We pray that you lead believers to
go and for us to be freely giving to those
who are going. In Jesus' name, amen.

CHAPTER 4

Turning Your Budget
Upside Down

I judge all things only by the price
they shall gain in eternity.
~ JOHN WESLEY

O ne of the most frequent questions I get asked when I begin challenging people to become part of the Giving Generation goes like this: "How much should I give?" The problem is, if you ask me, this is the wrong question. If the question is, "*How much?*" the questioner is looking to obey the letter of the law. The answer will always be the same: 10 percent.

But what if the question went like this: "How much *can* I give?" For example, if you knew it were possible to give away 90 percent of your income—and singlehandedly fund a program or nonprofit of your choice—wouldn't you want to do that? What if you knew that nobody in your church would ever have to struggle financially again because you were part of the Giving Generation? If you knew that hundreds or thousands of others would be inspired by your giving and join the movement too—how would that make you feel? This is the upside-down kingdom of heaven. It teaches us to stop thinking in the ways of the world and to start thinking in terms of heaven.

As a financial advisor, I see most people—Christians included—stuck on what I call the make-and-spend treadmill: making more so they can spend more, then needing to make even more to keep up with that spending. Making money accelerates the spending, which in turn must accelerate the making. It's a cycle that is never-ending, and it burns through energy and time. On that treadmill, we're only thinking about the present, the now, and how we're going to make up for last month's spending. When it comes to saving and giving, we don't have much money left over.

And it shows.

Most Americans give only 2 percent of their income to charity. Only a small percentage of Americans give anything away at all, and of that percentage, people give away only 2 percent of their income.

It gets worse.

If a 2 percent giving rate is alarming to you, the average savings rate of 6 percent should ring even more bells. From my experience in the finance industry, I can tell you that this is not enough to retire on, keep up a standard of living, or even cover major emergency expenses.

With only a combined 8 percent given to charity and to savings, we spend a total of 92 percent of our income on ourselves.

If you think of your spending like the food pyramid (which I showed you in the last chapter), America's current spending pyramid would look like this:

We spend most of our money on ourselves, siphon off a little for savings, and then give what's left, which is always miniscule, if anything at all. If we follow the money, we can see America cares about one major thing: our own enjoyment. For Americans, "living the good life" means spending as much as we make—and often spending more than we make.

This is not by mistake. The capitalist world we live in wants you to spend all of your time, resources, and talents on yourself because it is in the business of having you spend your entire income. Money in motion is what keeps the economy going. Does the economy care about your happiness or fulfillment? Hardly. The world and the devil have their own agendas.

Christians are no better than the rest of Americans. You might think that statistics among Christians would be different, but that's not the case at all. Across the board, finances look the same. We in the church give out of our own abundance. We trim the fat of the calf, giving it to God, but we refuse to sacrifice the golden calf, our idol of money.

Our currency says, *In God We Trust*. If we were honest, it would read, *In Us We Trust*.

We get angry over abortion and other political issues, but where is our anger at capitalism? It is selling us lies and leading to ungodly fin and finances. Our currency says, *In God We Trust*. If we were honest, it would read, *In Us We Trust*.

These are shocking statistics for all of us. We are generous people. We *intend* to give of our resources, but when we add up what we've given at the end of the year, we find we've actually donated very little. First, we spend on ourselves, then we save a little bit, then we spare what we can. As much as we want to share and help others, we end up giving sporadically, only when the moment presents itself and when we feel like we can afford it. When the offering plate comes around, we give what we can—which is minimal.

We are running, and we don't know how to slow the treadmill down.

The Fear That Keeps Us Running

When we look behind what's motivating the make-and-spend treadmill, what do we find powers it? My take is that it runs on fear. You may fall into one two camps: the FOFO (Fear of Future Outpacing) or the FOMO (Fear of Missing Out). The truth is, we *feel* like we don't have enough to give—and that feeling is strong. The reason it's so strong is that it's rooted in fear, one of the most gripping and motivating emotions. We fear that we'll need the money later, that we don't have enough or won't make enough in the future. We're worried we haven't saved enough.

Maybe, deep down, you know that you've spent beyond your means, and you're holding your breath for the next time the stock market dips or the next time your family asks everyone to get together for a destination wedding. You're already projecting what could go wrong, and you are worried because you're not sure if you have the room in your budget for one more thing.

The fear of what you might need in the future looms large: *What if I don't have enough for retirement? What if I don't have enough for my kids' college education? What if I need to make a shift in my work and need more savings? What if I should invest more?*

The make-and-spend treadmill has us on a fast run, and there's not a lot of wiggle room. We're exhausted and dreading an uptick in the speed.

Even more than that, it's a fear that we're not enough as we are. A voice says we need to spend more to keep up, to prove ourselves. When we can't keep up with the spending of our friends and neighbors, we fear what they will think of us, what our spending (or lack of spending) will say about us. It's FOMO, the fear of missing out. It's the fear of falling behind. This is the fear that keeps us jogging on that make-and-spend treadmill, running after our own worth but never getting any closer.

Fear is a powerful motivator; it's no wonder that marketers use it all the time to get us to buy their products. Insurance companies rely on your fear of getting in an accident, getting sick, or experiencing a natural disaster to get you to spend more on insurance. Car companies rely on your fear of being obsolete. Popular clothing brands rely on your fear of not being accepted or part of the club. We fear that we don't and won't have enough. We fear that we *aren't* enough as we are. Is that actually true?

You're not crazy for feeling the fear of not having enough. If you've spent most of what you have, you likely will need that final percentage in the bank, sooner than later, when an emergency hits or life happens. You are not wrong that life comes with expenses: as a financial advisor, I can't stress the importance of investing early enough and preparing for retirement.

Tell me this: Is keeping all your money for what "might" happen worth sacrificing the life that God has for you? Is it worth sacrificing a sense of purpose and peace? Is it worth the exhaustion that you feel?

Jesus said, "'Come to me, all who labor and are heavy laden, and I will give you rest. Take my yoke upon you, and learn from me, for I am gentle and lowly in heart, and you will find rest for your souls. For my yoke is easy, and my burden is light'" (Matthew 11:28–30). We are not meant to exhaust ourselves 24/7. We are not meant to be on the treadmill.

The big lie that keeps you running is that you aren't enough as you are. Social media regularly shows us our friends' new car, house, vacation, outfit, you name it. Every time you open your phone or turn on the TV, commercials and ads are everywhere you turn, telling you that your life is incomplete without consuming the next new thing. The discontentment is contagious. We struggle to succeed to try and fill this void, only to flaunt it in front of another, and the cycle goes on and on. Yet look at who Jesus spent His time with: children, lepers, tax collectors, and prostitutes (widely considered less than—outcasts and traitors—in that time), You don't have to meet any societal standard of wealth or status for Jesus to accept you or use you for kingdom purposes. You don't have to spend money for Jesus to bring you in.

When you believe that truth, it allows you to step off the treadmill and start actually making progress toward peace and purpose.

The question, then, is how do you start believing that you're enough?

To begin with, proclaim it as truth: You *are* enough. You are loved because of God's generosity. God gave His firstfruits. Abraham's obedience to be willing to sacrifice Isaac was a prophetic picture of what God was preparing to do for you on the cross. Christian, He sent Jesus to die on a wretched tree for you. Not for mankind—for *you*. He gave His first and best with Jesus for you. I am asking: Are you willing to sacrifice how you have been managing your money up until this point? I have a feeling, and studies show, that what you're clinging to isn't working anyway. You can let go and repent. Let's exchange it for a way of managing your money that puts God first and your wants last.

To do that, we're going to have to take an entirely different approach to finances, one that flips the current savings and spending pyramid on its head. My guess is that, if you're living in America, it will probably not be as painful as you think; you just might have your priorities in the wrong order.

The Christian Cashflow Continuum

To help you on your journey to become part of the Giving Generation, I want to help you take culture's plan for your money and flip it on its head. When we flip this me-first model upside down, we *begin* to see a glimmer of what God hopes and believes for us. When I lay this out for you, you might think I'm crazy. Remember that God's way always looks crazy through worldly lenses. The Giving Generation will defy what we think are the laws of what we imagine is possible.

What culture tells you is that, if you aren't rich, young, and powerful, you should keep trying harder. Find your passion? Maybe. Either way, you need to figure out why you haven't "made it" yet. If you're already rich and famous, make sure you keep it up. Don't lose your status. Don't fall behind that person who is *richer* or more prominent than you. There is always someone else to compare yourself to. And the comparison is relentless. The world's way will not stop until it steals every ounce of your peace and joy.

The world wants you to spend all of your time, resources, and talents on yourself because this is what keeps the hamster wheel moving. Money in motion is what keeps the economy going, but the world doesn't care about your happiness or fulfillment. It's no wonder the world is so shocked and surprised to see someone who pays it forward in the Starbucks line. If believers and unbelievers stand in wonderment when one person decides to buy someone's coffee behind them at Starbucks, imagine what they will do when they see the rise of the Giving Generation. One is a one-time generous act. The other is a lifestyle that sees nothing I own as "mine." This idea will inevitably make the bookshelves, the news channels, and the radio stations go wild.

When you look at where most of us (92 percent) spend our money, you will see that we work and live for *Me Inc*. If we follow the money, we can see that Americans care about one major thing, and that is our own enjoyment. Living like this is not only keeping you from the kingdom work God has planned for you—it's also making you miserable.

What I suggest is what I call the Christian Cashflow Continuum. It flips the worldly way on its head. God's way for you to use your money replaces the focus on making and spending with a focus on *saving* and

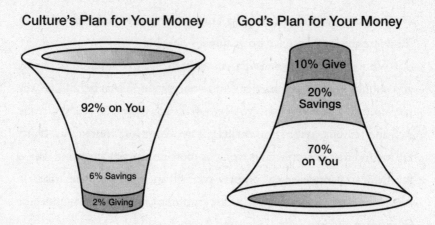

Culture's Plan for Your Money

God's Plan for Your Money

92% on You

6% Savings

2% Giving

10% Give

20% Savings

70% on You

giving. When you give and save first, you ensure that your life values are in the right place. You create purpose, rest, and stability in your life before turning to spending on yourself.

This new method turns the existing norm on its head. It takes the current prioritization of spending, which is: spending (92 percent), saving (6 percent), giving (2 percent), and flips the order: first priority as giving (10 percent), then saving (20 percent), and then spending (70 percent). When we give and save first, we'll find that we're able to give and save a whole lot more.

10 Percent for Eternity

Remember, the Bible doesn't say that "money is the root of all evil." No, it says that the *love* of money is the root of all kinds of evil. What you love will show itself by rising to the top of your finances. Therefore we start the Christian Cashflow Continuum with the money you put aside for eternity.

What you care most about should come first. What you value the most should be separated from the top first. If we chop the root off at the beginning, evil that stems from the love of money loses its power. If we give first, we strike at the heart issue with money. Sadly, most people tend to use people to get money. Instead, as Christians, we must reverse this; we must use money to get people. How do you "get" people? The gospel. The gospel is good news—that is, the truth that people cannot refute. It "gets" people to their core.

To be clear here, 10 percent is the *bare minimum*. The Bible acknowledges that the requirement for tithing is 10 percent. If we're flipping the worldly way on its head, we have to acknowledge that it might be possible for us to spend 10 percent on ourselves and 90 percent on saving and giving.

With God, anything is possible. God's goal for our life is not our mere satisfaction but our sanctification. This is why giving is first on the Christian Cashflow Continuum.

By giving first, you—
- Live into the fact that you don't have to "keep up" with anyone. You are striking at the heart of the issue saying, "The LORD is my shepherd; I shall not want .... My cup runneth over" (Psalm 23:1, 5 KJV).
- Cut off money's power at its source—it is no longer what you love the most, so it cannot control you.
- Step off the make-and-spend treadmill.
- Honor God and what He wants for your life.
- Find more fulfillment, joy, and purpose in every dollar you earn;
- Acknowledge the real One you worship.
- Put God back at the center of your life and trust Him with your finances.

What you value most comes first. To honor God first, use the *first* of what you make toward kingdom purposes.

_____

What you love will show

itself by rising to the top

of your finances.

_____

20 Percent Investing for the Future

The secondary priority in the Christian Cashflow Continuum is the 20 percent for long-term savings. I'm not talking about delayed spending by saving up for big purchases. I'm talking about retirement savings via a Roth IRA and/or 401(k) or another retirement savings vehicle.

Twenty percent is a lot, but, as a financial counselor, it's my rule of thumb. This money will help you receive the highest match on your 401(k), when applicable, and maximize your retirement accounts.

In my experience, much of the financial risk that investors take on is not motivated by the thrill of the chase for higher returns but instead motivated by necessity: the make-and-spend treadmill. So many Americans are not saving enough, so they are trying to "catch up" or get "back on track" through drastic and extremely risky bets. The sure-footed path is to cut back and save more over a longer period of time. If you save 20 percent, you don't have to worry about making more income or making a higher return because you already are saving a healthy amount. Starting early and saving the right percentage matters.

One note about emergency funds: if you haven't saved an emergency fund (six months of living expenses), then this needs to be the priority first. Use this 20 percent to build a healthy emergency fund before saving for retirement. This emergency fund will help relieve that feeling of gripping fear about the future: you know that, no matter what happens, you'll have a safety net. You'll have money for that unexpected repair or urgent care bill. You'll have money for the long tow or the hospital visit.

Let me be frank with you: the current savings rate of 6 percent reflects poorly on our country. We are not preparing for our own future. Compare this rate to other countries where the savings rate is more like 20 percent. We're sacrificing our future for the sake of temporary comforts.

If you're thinking, *How could I ever save 20 percent?* I hear you. There's no need to be overwhelmed. It may feel impossible for you to change overnight, but there are plenty of ways to grow in this area, whether or not you are still young.

What is 10 percent of your monthly income? What if an expense came along which cost that much money? Would you be able to pay for it? I believe that nearly every American could start saving at least 10 percent of their income.

How am I so sure? I compare savings to a tax increase: What would you do if (or what have you done when) you had to pay more to the federal government? If you're like most of us, you'd complain about it. Maybe you'd throw a pity party or vent about it to your spouse. Maybe you'd even threaten to leave the country. I'd bet almost anything that you'd still go to work the next day and pay those taxes.

Instead of waiting for the government to raise taxes to pay for social programs, why don't you tax yourself? Begin by trying to save at least 10 percent in the next sixty days. After that, work toward the savings sweet spot: 20 percent.

70 Percent Investing into Now, the Present

Notice that this category—the present—still accounts for the majority of your spending. It's okay to spend on yourself; it's necessary to spend on yourself in the present. You need food and clothing and supplies for your life, but putting "the present" last on the priority list keeps you content and fulfilled in your own life, as you build a life that matters. I can hear the critics whispering, "But what about taxes? I have to pay Aunt IRS." The neat thing with our tax code is that giving can reduce your taxes, and investing in certain investments may reduce or defer the current taxes you pay too. The tax code is designed to punish big income earners who are also big spenders, but it tends to benefit those who make giving and wise investing priorities.

With this 70 percent, I suggest creating a spending plan. I'm not a fan of traditional budgeting. (I'll talk about that more in a minute.) Without a plan, spending tends to get out of control, so frame it as a spending plan: How are you going to spend your money? To get a copy of our spending plan, go to RichYoungPowerful.com/spendingplan.[16]

Why Budgeting Doesn't Work

Let's face the facts: traditional budgeting rarely works. By budgeting, I don't mean the percentage-based method I've suggested here. I'm talking about line-item budgeting, tracking every purchase down to the dollar.

Financial pundits will say that you need to budget and watch every penny you spend. Budgets have as much success as your friend's fifth attempt to finally "get back in the gym." Budgets are like diets and New Year's resolutions. They start with good intentions and high morale, but they are consistently snuffed out by procrastination and lack of commitment.

We suspect they'll fail, and they often do.

Why do budgets fail so often? The reason is willpower. We live busy lives. The last thing we want to do before bed is to count up how much we spent that day. It takes a lot of effort and intentionality to look through our spending on a daily basis. It reminds me of "this week's trending diet." It requires a lot of extra work (shopping, cooking, and avoiding certain foods) and is not sustainable for the long run. Item-by-item budgeting isn't sustainable either.

Budgets also encourage us to focus on our limitations instead of our goals. Would any of you teach your son or daughter how to drive by telling them to focus on the guardrails? Of course not. Your driver-in-training would hit every guardrail down the highway, so why do we do this with finances? Why do we tell people to focus on the details of every expense, down to the final penny? You might spend hours poring over your bank statements, trying to make everything balance. It's time-consuming and exhausting.

Thankfully, there's a much better way to do this: the reordering of our finances through the Christian Cashflow Continuum.

Feel free to spend money on yourself—enjoy the blessings that God has provided you. What is the point of sowing without a season of reaping?

My opinion is that we need to stop budgeting and start changing our habits. Think about it: People who do anything consistently (keeping the weight off, for example) have learned to set their habits on autopilot. They have changed their habits by changing their own psychology. They have changed their identity, You are now a steward of your finances for God's will. That's exactly what this Christian Cashflow Continuum helps you do: put your finances on autopilot.

With your priorities in the right place, everything else will come naturally.

The Budget Solution: Artificial Scarcity

So if budgeting doesn't work—what *does*? Aside from using the Savings and Spending Pyramid I showed you in chapter 3, the technique I've found that works best for me and for my clients is what I call *artificial scarcity*.

When we give away 10 percent to the church or to charities, then save 20 percent, we're left with 70 percent of our income. What is 70 percent of your income? Use weekly or monthly numbers and compare it to the spending categories you've created above. Start with essentials and then move on to discretionary income. How much are you spending in that time period? Are you under that 70 percent dollar amount?

If not, it's time to make some difficult decisions. Maybe you downsize your house or car. Maybe you reconsider educational choices or leisure activities. Maybe you take more time to prepare meals at home. Whatever you need to do, get your spending down to 70 percent.

If you follow this formula, you won't need an item-by-item budget. You'll need a flexible retirement account, one that can keep up with how much you're pouring into it, because you're on the right track to success.

I'm not suggesting that you stop spending money on yourself. Some financial gurus will tell you to save everything you can—to live on a shoestring budget now so you can live like a king someday in the future. I don't believe in that, and I don't think it's biblical, either. Living in balance and enjoying every season is essential to a happy life. Ecclesiastes 3:1 says, "For everything there is a season, and a time for every matter under heaven." Feel free to spend money on yourself—enjoy the blessings that God has provided you. What is the point of sowing without a season of reaping?

Consider what a balanced financial life could look like for you. Instead of using a spending plan, practice artificial scarcity instead. Tracking your money is not necessary if you put first things first. However, if your spending goes off the rails every month, you need to institute your spending plan to ensure there is enough month at the end of the money, as Jim Rohn would say.[17]

Cheat God, Cheat Yourself

If you cheat God, you'll cheat yourself. If you can't manage to pull together 10 percent for giving, I honestly doubt that you're going to be

Sooner The Greater

Unsure how your savings could grow over time? See the chart below to help gain a better understanding of how your money can accumulate if you invest until age 65!*

Percentage of Income	Starting at AGE 20	AGE 25	AGE 30	AGE 35
5%	$1,043,565	$699,453	$465,255	$305,865
10%	$2,087,130	$1,398,905	$930,511	$611,729
15%	$3,130,696	$2,098,358	$1,395,766	$914,594
20%	$4,174,261	$2,797,810	$1,861,021	$1,223,459

able to save any money at all—for others or for yourself. You're stuck running on the make-and-spend treadmill, and it's getting you nowhere.

Let me share with you Eric and Michelle's story. Eric and Michelle are friends from my Bible study. They were making a combined $150,000 a year. After sitting down with them as a friend trying to help a friend professionally, I wanted to be careful what I said to protect our friendship foremost. They shared with me their one-page spending plan and I was shocked to see these devout believers tithing only $20 to $30 a week. Not surprisingly, when I got to the bottom of their finances and saw the investment column of what they were putting away for retirement—you guessed it. They were putting $150 a month in Eric's 401(k).

Luckily, Michelle asked for my advice and said, "Andrew, tell it how it is. How are we doing?" I pushed away from the table, leaned back in my chair, and chose my next words carefully. I looked at Eric and then at Michelle and said, "You are cheating your retirement by $2,350 every month, but worse yet, you're cheating God by $250 a week."

These friends were receptive to my thoughts, and after our conversation they began to take steps toward a healthier balance of giving, saving, and spending.

In addition to cheating God and cheating ourselves, a focus on making and spending doesn't leave any room for God's blessing. It doesn't allow opportunities for us to trust or for God to surprise us with good things. Instead, in fear, it motivates us to grab our blessings right away.

Make-and-spend leaves us fearful for our finances and our future, and, ultimately, it leaves us wondering if we will ever be enough. The reverse order of priorities has the opposite effect: it makes us confident and worry-free. We won't worry that we have enough because we've built a life within our own means. We won't worry that we aren't enough because we're less concerned about impressing people and more concerned about impressing God. We will be confident in our own future, and we will enjoy being able to share our financial blessings.

As we trust in God and build a life that matters, we will slowly realize that what burns away wasn't adding much to our lives in the first place.

Chapter 4: Reader's Guide

Biblical Text to Study	**Luke 6:38** *"Give, and it will be given to you: good measure, pressed down, shaken together, and running over will be put into your bosom. For with the same measure that you use, it will be measured back to you"* (NKJV).
Discussion	• In what ways do you experience fear around your finances? • Do you agree that how you spend your money can affect your testimony? • What did you think about the author's suggestion that budgets don't work? • Do you use a budget? • Where do you sit on the Christian Cashflow Continuum? • Is giving first on your list—or more like last? • In what ways might you be cheating God by the way you currently organize your finances?
Framework	**The Christian Cashflow Continuum** Go back to the CCC from this chapter and ask yourself what big changes need to be made in the way you save, spend, and give. What about small changes? How might your spending habits be sending a message you don't want to send?
Memorization	**Proverbs 11:25** *The generous soul will be made rich, and he who waters will also be watered himself* (NKJV).
Group Leader Questions	• Jesus makes guarantees that you will not leave house, home, and family for the gospel and not receive a hundredfold. Have you challenged Him on this?

Group Leader Questions	• Jesus has a tone of testing. Where else in scripture do we see this? • Those who are forgiven much, give much. Do you agree that your generosity = your gratitude? • How does our attitude of gratefulness and generosity connect with the passage from Matthew 18:21–35? • How does God's first move of generosity that we see in John 3:16, before the beginning of the universe, connect to our stewardship?
Action Item	Take our Philanthropy101 Class by going to Richyoungpowerful.com/programs. Plus, calculate 70 percent of your total income and ask yourself what it would look like to live on that amount rather than 100 percent.
Prayer	Lord, please renew my heart for your gospel, resurrection, and grace. For I approach you as a debtor with a debt that could not be paid off in a lifetime, even if I wanted to pay it off. I am grateful for how overwhelmingly your grace supplies. Amen.

CHAPTER 5

How to Cultivate the Habit of Generosity

If a person gets his attitude toward money straight,
it will help straighten out
almost every other area in his life.
~ BILLY GRAHAM

I f the last chapter felt intimidating to you—the idea that you have to flip your current spending and giving on its head—you'll love what I'm going to share with you now. Because no one goes from struggling to give to giving away half or more of their income overnight. It's certainly not plausible to believe that, if you only made more money, you'd give more money away. How do we grow as believers, as people, and become part of the Giving Generation? Easy. We think about generosity like a *garden.*

If you have grown up in church you have probably read or heard this parable before. Even if you have, I want you to pay close attention to it through the lens of giving generously.

In the Gospel of Matthew, Jesus used a garden as a metaphor for the spiritual life:

Then he [Jesus] told them many things in parables, saying: "A farmer went out to sow his seed. As he was scattering the seed, some fell along the path, and the birds came and ate it up. Some fell on rocky places, where it did not have much soil. It sprang up quickly, because the soil was shallow. But when the sun came up, the plants were scorched, and they withered because they had no root. Other seed fell among thorns, which grew up and choked the plants. Still other seed fell on good soil, where it produced a crop—a hundred, sixty or thirty times what was sown .... Listen then to what the parable of the sower means: When anyone hears the message about the kingdom and does not understand it, the evil one comes and snatches away what was sown in their heart. This is the seed sown along the path. The seed falling on rocky ground refers to someone who hears the word and at once receives it with joy. But since they have no root, they last only a short time. When trouble or persecution comes because of the word, they quickly fall away. The seed falling among the thorns refers to someone who hears the word, but the worries of this life and the deceitfulness of wealth choke the word, making it unfruitful. But the seed falling on good soil refers to someone who hears the word and understands it. This is the one who produces a crop, yielding a hundred, sixty or thirty times what was sown" (Matthew 13:3–8, 18–23 NIV).

We have all seen gardens that have been taken over by weeds. We shake our heads at the beauty of what once was. What used to be a beautiful, elegant, and purposefully tended garden now is a tangled web of weeds. A shadow of the straight line and symmetry of foliage that once was.

The new garden of weeds is useless to us because these weeds don't produce food for eating or flowers for looking at. They consume their surrounding resources without producing anything in return. They are a community of no fruit, no flowers, and no heavenly scent.

Jesus was fervent in warning us about the thorny weeds of the world. This part of the passage is worth reading again: "The seed falling among the thorns refers to someone who hears the word, but the worries of this life and the deceitfulness of wealth choke the word, making it unfruitful" (Matthew 13:22 NIV). In my perspective, financial worries are "the worries of this life." "The deceitfulness of wealth" is exactly what leads us to make excuses for not giving. We think we need more. We think we need to hold on to our wealth.

To combat these weeds takes maintenance of your financial garden.

How to Cultivate a Beautiful Garden

Maybe it's because I'm a financial advisor, or maybe it's because it's human nature, but clients and readers always want to know what this means practically, as far as their giving. They want to know, essentially, "Okay, if I'm being faithful with what God has given me, how much, where, and how should I be giving?"

To answer that question, I walk clients through the Give Now flowchart on the following page.

Give Now

The best way to get started is to take a leap of faith and give now. In my experience, this is the most difficult part. People like the *idea* of generosity

but often find excuses not to give. Maybe you've heard someone say, "If I won the lottery, I would give a lot of it away." But the if/then dynamic will not grow a garden. We can't wait for the ideal environment to grow. We are the gardeners. We have to create the ideal environment for growth. Besides hoping to win the lottery, here are the many other ways we tend to put off the start of giving. We say things like:

"I'm not as rich as my friends, so I can't afford to give yet."
We all do this in various ways. We compare ourselves to those around us, and sometimes that comparison turns into justification as to why we can't give. Do you believe your friends are financially more secure than you? Don't be so sure. In 1954, Leon Festinger developed the social comparison theory. His study showed that when you compare yourself to others, you typically compare yourself to outliers, either positive or negative. We think, "I am not that bad of a person—compared to my neighbor, who's a real sinner." We do the same thing financially. When we say, "I don't make that much each year," or, "I don't have that much saved," we're thinking of the richest people we know.

We're comparing ourselves to outliers. *I'm not as rich as my Uncle Conrad—now that is a rich family.* These exact trains of thought pull us out of the will to give because we aren't "that rich."

The bottom line is, you *are* rich. Pull out last year's tax return. How much do you make a year? Then calculate how much you make a day. Did you know that 10 percent of the world lives on two dollars or less per day?[18] It's hard to fathom the hardships billions of others endure, yet we worry about how we are going to make our own ends meet.

"I'm still not making enough."
Many young professionals have shot back at me and said, "Andrew, I am not making enough!" My response is, "Have you asked for a raise?" Maybe you have asked for a raise but were rejected. I give these people a challenge: Can you give 120 percent to your work for the next 90 days? Can you come in early? Stay late? Extend yourself for your coworker? Go above and beyond for your leaders? Do everything from extra projects to picking up trash on your way down the hall?

See what happens then. If your own supervisors don't notice, I bet one of your vendors or clients will. If no one in your vicinity notices, put your resume out there for a higher-paying job: you are a better employee now than you were ninety days ago, and you'll have the confidence to go work for the next organization with the rigor you gave your last organization.

For others, a side hustle might be the better option. Or maybe it's time to move, sell a car, or find another way to decrease expenses. Work to get to a place where you can cover the basics and still give.

"I don't have the money."
If you don't have the money, then you don't have the money. Why is this the case? Is it because you've spent all of your money on yourself? Have you prioritized your wants and greed before giving to God or saving for your future? You might not be able to give 10 percent of your paycheck

today. How can you start changing your lifestyle and spending habits so that you're not out of money at the end of the month?

"If I invest the money now, I'll have more to give later."
What this excuse implies is that we can outperform God. God knows what is best for the world and best for your life: trust God with your money *now*. Trust that God will bring a better profit from it than the market ever could. Right now is the time to give. God can make a better return on your giving. Spend your life being a part of His work.

"I have to pay off my debt first."
Some financial pundits are dogmatic about debt being the enemy. If debt is the enemy, then why do so many wealthy individuals use debt?

To be clear, there is a difference between debt and toxic debt. There is a difference between being *in* debt and *having* debt. If you have $100,000 in a checking account and $100,000 in mortgage debt, you have debt but financially speaking, you are not *in* debt. You have enough to cover the debt tomorrow, if need be.

There is a difference between debt and toxic debt.

Consumer debt, cars, and any debt that is connected to a depreciating asset should be minimized quickly: these are classic examples of toxic or "bad" debt. What's best is to stay out of this kind of debt in the first place. I understand, you had emergency expenses and there were surprises you didn't account for. Maybe someone needed medical attention or lost a job. That all is important and true.

I'm not speaking about specific times you overspent or the surrounding circumstances; I'm asking about trends over time. Do you consistently overspend or consistently stay within your means?

In my experience as a financial advisor, the most consistent and defining feature of those who stay out of debt is the commitment to live within one's means. They plan for surprises and prepare for financial winters.

Matthew 6:24 says, "No one can serve two masters, for either he will hate the one and love the other, or he will be devoted to the one and despise the other. You cannot serve God and money." Many, including myself, have interpreted this verse in a way that lets themselves off the hook. They say, "I am not rich, nor do I spend my time trying to become rich. I am not serving money. This scripture isn't for me." But take a second look: Could this verse apply to your toxic debt? Isn't paying off debt only another way to serve money? Debt is akin to fire. Fire can be used constructively to keep us warm or it can be used destructively. Debt can help us if we use it in contained, controlled ways. But it can also be dangerous—and it can burn our gardens to the ground if we let it.

Should you wait to tithe until you are completely debt-free? No way. No matter if you have good debt, bad debt, or no debt at all, giving and tithing and saving must be prioritized as nonnegotiables. If you have bad debt getting in the way of these priorities, it's time to try something new until you are free of toxic debt.

Debt is not the biggest hurdle to a generous life. You can get out of financial debt. However, if you are serving your material things—addicted to getting more and more—that will be much harder to overcome. Even if you find a way to be debt-free according to the bank, yet refuse to love God and love others, then you are bankrupt with the Creator of the universe.

"I don't understand why I need to tithe."
Is it that we *have* to be generous, or that we *get* to be generous? Listen to the scripture below: "But who am I, and what is my people, that we

————

Even if you find a way to be

debt-free according to the bank,

yet refuse to love God and love

others, then you are bankrupt

with the Creator of the universe.

————

should be able thus to offer willingly? For all things come from you, and of your own have we given you" (1 Chronicles 29:14). We get to give out of our abundance because we are blessed. It might not feel that way immediately, but as you step out in faith, you will see that helping others is its own reward.

Give Often

The practice of giving is like working out: if it's going to change us, it has to be done consistently, and yet I still hear every excuse in the book:

"We give when we feel led to give."
There's nothing wrong with soul-searching. As I've already shown you, it's important to make sure that your money is going toward kingdom purposes and that the causes are ones in which you want to invest. But so often, this line is used simply to avoid giving at all. If we don't follow up this sentiment with research, then what we're really saying is that we don't care to give.

If we're looking for a sign as to whether we should give or not, we don't need to look any further than the Bible. Giving is a practice which is commanded; it's not something that we do when we're in the mood.

"I already give some."
Ignorance of the truth leaves room for spiritual growth but delusion is dangerous in a believer's walk with Christ. As the secular philosopher Mark Twain once said "It ain't what you don't know that gets you into trouble. It's what you know for sure that just ain't so." Let me point you towards the facts with the utmost charity that we aren't generous but far from it. We believe we are, but it just ain't so.

How Generous I am with Money, by Generation

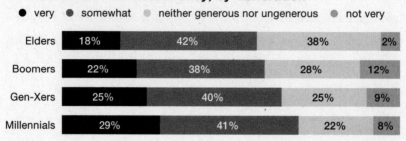

	very	somewhat	neither generous nor ungenerous	not very
Elders	18%	42%	38%	2%
Boomers	22%	38%	28%	12%
Gen-Xers	25%	40%	25%	9%
Millennials	29%	41%	22%	8%

"I must take care of my family first."

Yes, as responsible adults, it is important to cover the basics for those in your care: water, electricity, food, and shelter. Those who find themselves unable to pay their rent have bigger challenges to tackle than figuring out how to give financially. Is that really your situation? Or can you afford eating out, new clothes, and other small luxuries? If so, then it's my opinion that you have enough to start helping those around you. If you are putting first things first, I believe that is when Matthew 6:25–34 comes to life. The Lord will provide if you have the right order in place. Trust that God cares just as much about your family as you do. In fact, God cares more.

"I don't feel like giving."

You may have heard this verse from 2 Corinthians: "Each one must give as he has decided in his heart, not reluctantly or under compulsion, for God loves a cheerful giver" (2 Corinthians 9:7). Sometimes when people quote this verse, they use their emotional state as an excuse not to give. They say, "I wouldn't be giving cheerfully." They base their giving habits on the whim of the moment: how generous or cheerful they are feeling.

Yet this Bible verse is often misinterpreted, and the excuse isn't biblical. Cheerfulness isn't a prerequisite to giving; in fact, it is often a result. I think you'll find that generosity is the process which transforms you into that gleeful person: you become a kinder, more loving, more purpose-filled version of yourself as you give. Giving is not a result of a changed heart—it is the means of a changed heart. Become a person who gives regularly, and through that practice you will become more cheerful. If you are waiting to become cheerful before you give, you may wait a very long time. When you are obedient, your joy will grow.

"I forget to give."

If you honestly struggle with forgetfulness, you're in luck: automated giving is a simple solution. You can give to your church or another organization straight from your paycheck or checking account.

Often, forgetfulness is actually an avoidance technique. Giving can be difficult at first, but as the practice transforms your life, you will find it brings you purpose and joy. My hope is that, by now, you're starting to see how important giving is, for your personal life, for your church, and for your Christian witness to the world. It's going to take some personal change, but it will be worth it.

Give Forever

I mean this in two ways. First, we never stop giving. We're not looking for a quotient to fill. Our duty of giving isn't capped at any specific number. Giving is not something to ever finish doing. Giving is a practice which changes us and can help others around us, and it is a transformation which is never done.

I also mean "forever" in that our giving can have an eternal impact. Think of the kind of impact the money you have has on the world around you: your giving has a domino effect. As people's lives improve, and as they experience the love of Christ, they will be able to spread that love too.

The more you give, the easier it will become. My hope for you is that, as you continue to give, you'll find it addicting. You'll want to give more and more. Here are a few practical suggestions on how to give more than you're giving now.

STEP 1: Make It Automatic

Set up bank drafts or another form of automated payments. The less you have to think about your giving, the easier it is. You can bypass the struggle of deciding each month to transfer the money. You only have to make the decision to be obedient once, and then it happens automatically.

STEP 2: Utilize Windfall Opportunities

Occasionally, we are fortunate enough to receive chunks of money. The best example of this is during tax season. The average tax refund in 2021 was $2,775.[19] The data shows that most Americans making six figures don't give even that much to charity in a given year.

Very few saved their tax return for long-term investments, and fewer still gave their tax return away. What I have found with clients is that large tax returns have become a delayed spending tactic. Studies have shown that a majority of families' tax returns are used for the following:

+ making large purchases
+ paying off debts
+ short-term savings (keyword: short-term)
+ everyday expenses

Instead of using your tax return as "delayed spending," try giving it away.

Tax returns aren't the only windfall you might receive. After a promotion, raise, or large liquidity event like receiving an inheritance or selling a business, you might have a chunk of cash on your hands. What if the next time you received an unexpected bonus, a promotion, or a raise, you decided not to consume it but to give it? Pray to God and speak with your family about setting aside 50 percent (or all) of your next raise—or the next percentage of a bonus or other windfall—toward your giving.

STEP 3: Make Incremental Changes

Asking believers to jump with both feet into tithing 10 percent works for those who are able to make radical shifts. For others, they can be overwhelmed at the idea of making drastic changes. I want to challenge you: Set a reminder on your calendar and phone to increase your automatic tithe by 1 percent every six months. I don't know many families that could not achieve that goal.

Incremental changes would force you to slowly make reductions in your spending, investing, or anything that gets in the way of building a meaningful life through giving. You can go from 0 percent to 10 percent in five years.

Another simple way to increase your giving is to withhold less from your paycheck during the year. You won't get a tax refund, but you'll have better cashflow during the year, and you can direct any "extra" money that you're getting per month toward a church or charity.[20]

STEP 4: Tithe Exponentially

My absolutely favorite way to increase your giving is to practice exponential tithing. You may have heard about the power of compound interest, but what if you could use this same phenomenon to increase your tithing? The key is understanding the difference between simple and compound interest.

The easiest example of simple interest is your mortgage. Your taxes and insurance may change, but your actual mortgage payment is static

How U.S. Family Incomes Have Grown Since the 1950s

Real Mean and median family income in the U.S. (in 2017 CPI-U-RS adjusted dollars)

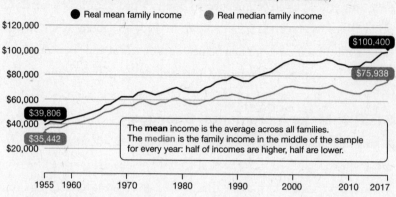

over the term of the loan. This is why your 30-year mortgage (if you do not refinance) will be the same payment the entire period.

Compound interest works slightly differently.

Let's take the example of increase in income over time. Did you know that for most Americans, incomes over a career have increased anywhere from 6 to 12 percent? As you can see in the graph above if you take the median income in 1967 of $2,464 a year and compare it to the 2009 value of $26,530, the average increase is 5.82 percent over 42 years.

When I ask clients to compare what they made as a twenty-two-year-old to what they make now, as fifty-five-year-olds, the response is usually along these lines: "I graduated in 1977 and landed a job making $13,500 and now I make $98,000." With a quick interest calculation, that equals 6.44 percent.

I have surveyed countless families who told me that if they took their entry job pay right out of college and compared it to the highest salary of their career, they would see a 6 to 12 percent rate of growth over their career. Isn't that amazing? The only problem is that most people are spending these increases on themselves.

Year	Income	Mortgage Balance	18% of Income	Fixed Payment	Excess Income	% Tithing
1	$ 100,000	$ 342,693	$18,000	$18,000	$0	0.00%
2	$ 103,000	$ 335,163	$18,540	$18,000	$540	0.52%
3	$ 106,090	$ 327,405	$19,096	$18,000	$1,096	1.03%
4	$ 109,273	$ 319,410	$19,669	$18,000	$1,669	1.53%
5	$ 112,551	$ 311,172	$20,259	$18,000	$2,259	2.01%
6	$ 115,927	$ 302,684	$20,867	$18,000	$2,867	2.47%
7	$ 119,405	$ 293,938	$21,493	$18,000	$3,493	2.93%
8	$ 122,987	$ 284,925	$22,138	$18,000	$4,138	3.36%
9	$ 126,677	$ 275,638	$22,802	$18,000	$4,802	3.79%
10	$ 130,477	$ 266,069	$23,486	$18,000	$5,486	4.20%
11	$ 134,392	$ 256,209	$24,191	$18,000	$6,191	4.61%
12	$ 138,423	$ 246,049	$24,916	$18,000	$6,916	5.00%
13	$ 142,576	$ 235,580	$25,664	$18,000	$7,664	5.38%
14	$ 146,853	$ 224,793	$26,434	$18,000	$8,434	5.74%
15	$ 151,259	$ 213,677	$27,227	$18,000	$9,227	6.10%
16	$ 155,797	$ 202,223	$28,043	$18,000	$10,043	6.45%
17	$ 160,471	$ 190,421	$28,885	$18,000	$10,885	6.78%
18	$ 165,285	$ 178,260	$29,751	$18,000	$11,751	7.11%
19	$ 170,243	$ 165,729	$30,644	$18,000	$12,644	7.43%
20	$ 175,351	$ 152,817	$31,563	$18,000	$13,563	7.73%
21	$ 180,611	$ 139,512	$32,510	$18,000	$14,510	8.03%
22	$ 186,029	$ 125,803	$33,485	$18,000	$15,485	8.32%
23	$ 191,610	$ 111,676	$34,490	$18,000	$16,490	8.61%
24	$ 197,359	$ 97,120	$35,525	$18,000	$17,525	8.88%
25	$ 203,279	$ 82,121	$36,590	$18,000	$18,590	9.15%
26	$ 209,378	$ 66,666	$37,688	$18,000	$19,688	9.40%
27	$ 215,659	$ 50,741	$38,819	$18,000	$20,819	9.65%
28	$ 222,129	$ 34,332	$39,983	$18,000	$21,983	9.90%
29	$ 228,793	$ 17,423	$41,183	$18,000	$23,183	10.13%
30	$ 235,657	$ -	$42,418	$18,000	$24,418	10.36%

Take John Doe. He is a bright thirty-year-old who has a desire to contribute and be more obedient in his faith. John makes $100,000 a year and tithes $0. He purchased a home for $350,000 with a 30-year mortgage at 3 percent interest. His payment is $1,500 (rounded up), which equates to 18 percent of his pay. John is doing quite well for someone fairly new to his career.

With all this data in mind, what if John froze the 18 percent in relation to his income? If John became disciplined enough to distribute 18 percent of earnings, regardless of any bonuses or pay increases, an interesting thing occurs. The mortgage payment stays fixed while his income slowly increases annually at 3 percent. Therefore, John, over time, creates a spread between the 18 percent of his income and fixed mortgage payment. This surplus can then be rerouted into his tithing fund.

Over time, John's small sacrifice creates a true transformation. During a span of thirty years, we took someone from not tithing at all to giving over 10 percent of his gross income—from tithing $0 to almost $24,000 a year.

That's a marked improvement!

This technique alone can change you and your family's life and be a great blessing to your own life. We are not saying this is enough, because our goal is 10 percent as a minimum. Remember, this is only one strategy to get you there.

The Gardener's Love for the Garden

No gardener invites destructive weeds into their garden; weeds show up unannounced and uninvited. They thrive off seemingly nothing. You can count on weeds to show up—it's only a matter of time. A loving gardener plans for these weeds to come, sees when they're there, and is willing to get down on hands and knees in order to make sure they don't choke out the beauty of the garden.

How much attention are you giving your financial garden?

You don't have to go searching for financial worries. We have all experienced "worry-weeds" sprouting up in the gardens of our minds—and even toxic debt sprouting up in the gardens of our financial lives. It is natural to have weeds pop up and challenge our resolve.

When it comes to the garden of your financial life, don't let excuses choke out the fruit that is possible for you. Have the diligence and commitment to eliminate the weeds before they mature and spread. Treat your generosity like a garden and weed out everything which holds you back from joining the Giving Generation. As I'll show you in the next chapter, you'll be thrilled at what can grow.

Chapter 5: Reader's Guide

Biblical Text to Study: Leviticus 27:30 and Genesis 4:1–16

Discussion
- Do you think of your tithes as holy?
- Where do financial worries originate? How can our perspective on firstfruits help or hurt our worries?
- Why does order matter in the Bible? Can you think of other ways order has mattered in the Bible? For example, Abraham with Isaac.
- What is the difference between Cain's and Abel's sacrifices? How does the order they treat bringing their sacrifice affect the sacrifice?
- How can we practically place our tithe first in our spending plan?

Framework   **Give Now Flowchart**
Go back to the Give Now flowchart and ask yourself: Which area needs your attention? Are you giving now? Are you giving often? What would it look like for you (and your family) to give forever?

Memorization   **Proverbs 3:9** *Honor the LORD with your wealth and with the firstfruits of all your produce.*

Action Items
- If you are getting a large tax refund, consult your CPA/tax preparer about adjusting your tax withholding so you can begin giving more to your church each month.

- Set a reminder on your phone calendar every six months to increase your tithe by 1 percent.
- Next pay raise or promotion: be sure to split the difference. (e.g., with a 3 percent raise, increase your standard of living by 1.5 percent and increase your tithe by 1.5 percent.)

Prayer   Lord, search my heart. Am I putting you first in my finances? Father, help me to be generous as an overflow of the gratitude and grace you have shared with me, your servant. Help me not to check the box that I am tithing. How can I grow closer to you through offerings and giving? In Jesus' name, Amen

Setting a Limit on Your Worth

He is no fool who gives what he cannot keep
to gain what he cannot lose.
~ JIM ELLIOT

I once met a businesswoman who was a wealthy entrepreneur. She had a profitable business. One evening as she was counting up her net worth and achievements, she thought to herself, *I already have a Mercedes, multiple rental properties, a beach house, and a nice retirement nest egg put aside. But my business keeps growing! What am I supposed to do with all of this wealth?*

She laughed to herself as she thought, *I'll buy more houses, put more in my retirement accounts.*

Just like her goal of one million had become ten million, her goal of ten million became 100 million. She thought, *Once I have $100 million, I will finally have everything I want, and with that much money, I'll never* run out. *I can relax, travel, and stay anywhere I want, buy even more cars if I decide, eat at the most exclusive, fanciest restaurants . . . and then I'll be happy.*

Then I'll be happy.

Now, you may or may not be able to relate to this woman in terms of the amount she was making. But I've yet to meet anyone who doesn't relate to the "then I'll be happy" attitude.

Although we all generally agree with the maxim that money can't buy happiness, we don't live like we believe this is true. We find ourselves constantly striving for more and more and more, always promising ourselves that the striving will stop when we get to the fill-in-the-blank destination. Then that destination comes, and of course, we keep on striving.

When will enough be enough?

Jesus taught a parable about a man who gathered up riches for himself, and He clearly called this man out as a fool. The Gospel of Luke says:

> And he told them a parable, saying, "The land of a rich man produced plentifully, and he thought to himself, 'What shall I do, for I have nowhere to store my crops?' And he said, 'I will do this: I will tear down my barns and build larger ones, and there I will store all my grain and my goods. And I will say to my soul, "Soul, you have ample goods laid up for many years; relax, eat, drink, be merry"'" (Luke 12:16–19).

Two thousand years later this sounds like the original recipe for the American Dream: keep on accumulating. Once you have accumulated a good-sized crop, the next practical thing is to build a barn to hoard these newfound riches.

The problem is that you always have to build bigger barns.

As an ambitious entrepreneur, I have set goals, and I have achieved them. Over and over again, the feeling of success faded fast. I only celebrated for a brief moment before plotting new goals and setting new deadlines.

Can you relate? Did you ever dream that you would live in the house you reside in today? Can you remember a time you only dreamed of the retirement balance you have now? After graduating college did you imagine you would make the income you presently do?

Even so, we dream of second homes, bigger balances, better salaries. We are ambitious people. We relate to this driven farmer who reaped bountifully. How quickly we all lose our joy, turning to the next barn to be built. Notice that the rich fool is talking to *himself*. He's not praying or asking God's input. The end of that parable does not turn out so well for him:

> "But God said to him, 'Fool! This night your soul is required of you, and the things you have prepared, whose will they be?' So is the one who lays up treasure for himself and is not rich toward God" (Luke 12:20–21).

It's no different today. If I could speak candidly to the successful businesswoman, I would remind her, "Someone else is going to enjoy your wealth after you." I often tell my clients to get busy traveling, enjoy their retirement, and give their money away now. Why? Because if they don't, their kids might be the ones flying first class instead and giving their money to all kinds of things they disagree with. I am encouraging you to begin "giving while you're living so you're knowing where it's going."

A Caretaker of Wealth

Some may read this parable and think that God condemns riches. I disagree. The Lord loves to see people stewarding their wealth well. But being a good caretaker of wealth does not mean hoarding it. A steward understands that none of our resources actually belong to us; all of our assets belong to God. They are just on loan, and they are to be carefully looked after. Stewards live in confidence that their resources are God's to give and God's to take away.

> **A steward understands that none of our resources actually belong to us.**

As a financial advisor, I have learned from wise investors ranging from fifty years old to one hundred and four years old. What I have discovered is that most people who were frugal and have saved a fortune did it for one reason: fear. They were worried about being poor again. They were worried they would lose it all or their family would go without. Despite having millions of dollars, they still couldn't shake the fear of being without.

When we find ourselves hoarding, might we consider that it's because we're afraid of losing what we believe to be ours? We store up because of fear. We build bigger barns, but what do we have to show for it? The truth is, we're afraid of losing the wealth we've worked so hard to attain, even when we know we don't need it.

The even harder truth is this: it's weighing us down.

This life of hoarding is not what Christians are called to. We are not called to build bigger and bigger barns—and, honestly, is that even what we want? Wealth we don't use?

Neither are we called to live in fear. In 2 Timothy we read, "For God gave us a spirit not of fear but of power and love and self-control" (1:7). Fortunately, there is more to life than gathering wealth and, even better, we do not have to live in fear.

For those of you looking to build bigger barns, I have a challenge. What if you said, "That's enough for me"?

What if you set a barn limit?

Materialism is the familiar disorder of going around saying, "I see it, and I want it." Motivating the hoarding culture is that familiar fear that I don't have enough and that I am not enough. The only antidote is generosity. This is the only way to grow in contentment, and it's the only way to join the Giving Generation.

With the courage to say, "This is enough," you give yourself the ability to do much more for your own life and for others with your money. "Enough" is a forgotten word in our vocabulary. As believers in Christ, let's revive it. Let us explore together what might be possible when we dare to say: It's enough. I am enough. I have enough.

Live Your Life Like a Charity

Did you know that Rick Warren, the retired pastor of Saddleback Church in California, gives away 91 percent of his income? For over 30 years he increased his tithe by 1 percent or more. When *The Purpose Driven Life* sold millions of copies, he and his wife, Kay, decided to give 91 percent of their income away. He stopped taking a salary from his church and even paid back all that Saddleback Church had ever paid him.

I once heard Warren say that he had been playing "a game" with God: he would give to God, and God would give to him, and they'd see who won. He noted that he lost for thirty years straight! What a challenging perspective.

David Platt, an author and the lead pastor at McLean Bible Church in Vienna, Virginia, gives away the royalties for his book *Radical*. Francis Chan, author and founding pastor of Cornerstone Community Church in Simi Valley, California, downsized his home and his lifestyle in order to better serve his community and demonstrate how to live out the gospel. In an interview, speaking about the downsizing and the opportunities he has to give to other people, he said, "I've never felt happier."[21]

John Wesley, eighteenth-century Anglican preacher and founder of the Methodist movement, preached that Christians should only live on what they absolutely need, giving away all excess money. When he began tracking his own expenses, at first he was only able to give away 6 percent of his income: 28 pounds for himself, 2 pounds to give away. Through the years, and as he wrote more and gained notoriety, Wesley began earning a significant income. Instead of increasing his standard of living, he gave away the rest, until the percentages were entirely flipped: he was living on 2 percent of his income and giving away the remaining 98 percent.[22]

I call this living your life like a charity. A charity uses necessary resources to keep up their facilities and programs, but they aren't looking to accumulate funds. Instead, they use all extra money toward helping those they serve.

What if we, too, lived that way? What if we managed our finances like that of nonprofits? Would we live our lives differently? Instead of building barns and bigger barns, what if we took what we needed and gave the rest away? What if we lived off of a decent salary and put the excess toward something that would make a lasting difference in the world?

Most of us in America have more than we need for ourselves. Instead of chasing after "more," can we stop accumulating and start giving? If we

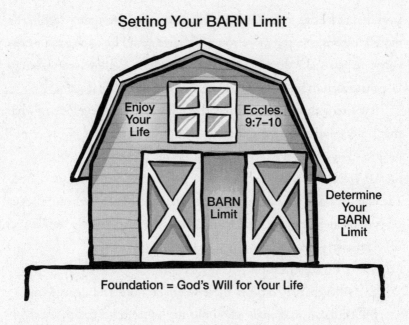

Setting Your BARN Limit

Enjoy Your Life

Eccles. 9:7–10

BARN Limit

Determine Your BARN Limit

Foundation = God's Will for Your Life

were going to do this, it would start with defining a financial life that suits us well—and then committing to giving the rest away.

Building a Solid Financial Barn

Rather than building barns and barns of extras, what would it look like to create a financial "barn" that met your needs and didn't hoard a bunch of extra? You might have a little bit set aside for a rainy day—but you don't have an unlimited amount of storage to keep growing and growing extras that you don't need or use. You keep what you need—and you give the rest away.

This is what I call *setting the barn limit*.

What's incredible is that when you set your own barn limit, you are stewarding your finances according to God's will, and He is stewarding your financial worries. "The LORD will command the blessing on you in your barns and in all that you undertake. And he will bless you in the land that the LORD your God is giving you" (Deuteronomy 28:8). The more He gives you, the more you get to give away! Imagine a life where you were like Rick Warren or David Platt or John Wesley and you got to be generous with hundreds of thousands or millions of dollars.

It starts with setting your own barn limit. Let's take a look at what that process looks like from the ground up.

Step 1: The Foundation

The foundation of your barn, like the foundation of your life, must be set on your obedience to Christ. Here's how Jesus expressed it in the Gospel of Matthew:

> "Everyone then who hears these words of mine and does them will be like a wise man who built his house on the rock. And the rain fell, and the floods came, and the winds blew and beat on that house, but it did not fall, because it had been founded on the rock. And everyone who hears these words of mine and does not do them will be like a foolish man who built his house on the sand" (7:24–26).

In light of this, when we're instructed to give, we build that foundation by giving a percentage of our income first. When we build our finances on this obedience, we build our barn on a rock, a firm foundation.

So many people build their barns on unstable ground, on sinking sand. They build it on other people's expectations or on society's pressures. That kind of foundation is ever-shifting. It never holds you up. Jesus' commandments in His Word and God's call on your life are solid.

Step 2: The Walls

The walls of your barn are your spending limits. As much as our capitalistic economy would have you believe otherwise, you do not have to spend everything you make. Setting limits is tough, but it is something everyone can do.

People don't like setting spending limits; it makes them feel like they don't have a choice. The funny thing about limits is that taking care of yourself and putting some boundaries on your spending actually empowers you to have more freedom. Let me explain how.

When you're on that make-and-spend treadmill, you'll face financial emergencies over and over again. You will feel like a victim of your circumstances. You wouldn't have that emergency if you prepared. And how you can prepare is by learning to set limits on your spending.

Limiting yourself helps you to become a better money manager in the long run, someone who is not ruled by the bills and paycheck of the current month, but who can make long-term decisions, ride out tough times, and take advantage of opportune moments with confidence. If you don't set a limit for your income spending, the world will always have a larger and faster hamster wheel for you to run on.

What sacrifices and active steps can you take to give more in the next thirty days? Here are a few ideas to jump-start your thinking:

- Can you downsize your home?
- Can you sell things in your home? Would an estate sale help you downsize?
- Can you commute with only one car?
- Can you sell your new car and buy an older one?

Build your walls, and you will be able to withstand financial storms.

Step 3: The Roof

The final step in the process is completely countercultural, but one I believe, for many Americans, could bring endless amounts of peace and joy. That is to set an income cap for yourself. You read that right: set a limit for how much you make every year. Your income cap is the roof of your barn.

What do you want for yourself and your family? How much is your baseline for the lifestyle you desire either now or when you retire? What are your financial goals? How much do they cost?

Here are some examples of financial goals:

+ Pay off the house.
+ Save a certain amount for retirement.
+ Retire by a certain age.
+ Put money toward children and grandchildren's education.
+ Buy a vacation home.

With that list in front of you, ask yourself, "What income would provide that?"

The goal here is to draw a line in the sand, to finally say, "I have enough." As you write the list, pray. Pray for discernment to know which items will help you serve God and live life well, and which ones you're supposed to give up.

Is it crazy? It's unusual. For those of us contemplating building more and more, bigger and bigger barns, it can actually be a relief—a way off the treadmill. It's a way to create purpose and to stop trying to perform for everyone else.

Building a roof is so crucial because it changes the operative question around generosity from "How much should I *give?*" to "How much should I *keep?*" Instead of determining what income you give, you set a limit to what income you keep—and the rest you give back to God.

We have to balance between God's will for our life and our dreams. By setting a barn limit that includes our bucket list items, we can stop moving the bar. When you stop moving the bar, you will finally be free. Soon you will be giving away more than you ever dreamed possible.

The world will tell you that you can always have more money, that more is always better. But if you actually want to create the best (and most impactful) life that you can, you'll need to give that money away. No one ever said you have to stop at giving 10 percent. As you give more of yourself and your income, you will walk even more closely with God.

Finally Enough

People may think, "This is going to be one boring life if I have to cap my income and follow only God's will for my life." In my perspective, there's nothing more boring than a meaningless life: one with the same empty pursuits on repeat. Believe me, you can tire of spending money on yourself.

Ordinary, inexpensive pursuits are often the most fulfilling: relationships, time spent with others, rest, and taking care of your mind, spirit, and body. It's the thrills and extra experiences that wear out after a time.

Apart from what's actually meaningful to us (our faith, our relationships, helping our community), there is not much excitement in a life of money, fame, and power. It's a monotonous and endless path: possessions and experiences centered around ourselves will never fill us up. The thrill becomes more and more difficult to attain. How can we ever arrive financially if we constantly move the line in the sand? We won't.

Let God's call on your life draw the line in the sand. Let God tell you when enough is enough—and give the rest away. In doing so, you will experience the rest and reward you've been hoping for, and you will achieve the meaningful life you've been wanting.

————

Let God tell you when enough

is enough—and give the rest

away. In doing so, you will

experience the rest and reward

you've been hoping for.

————

Chapter 6: Reader's Guide

Biblical Text to Study: Luke 12:12–28

Discussion	• Were you and your family able to come up with a barn limit? • What does your family really need financially to meet your needs? • Have you made plans lately without praying over them? Is God integrated into your plans?

Framework

Setting the Barn Limit
Go back to the "setting the barn limit" exercise and, if you didn't already, set your own barn limit. Decide what you need to live on to meet your needs, and ask God what He wants to do with the rest.

Memorization

Luke 12:15 *And He said to them, "Take heed and beware of covetousness, for one's life does not consist in the abundance of the things he possesses"* (NKJV).

Group Leader Questions

• How did pride bewitch the Rich Fool?
• How can we avoid finding confidence in the provision instead of the provider?
• How do these scriptures connect with James 4:13–15?
• Can you remember a time when you desired, planned, and hoped for something to happen? Once it occurred, how long did your contentment last?
• How can we verbalize our need for God? Begin using short prayers such as, "Jesus, this is in your hands." Begin to finish your sentences with, "...God willing."

Action Items

- Go through the list of the following suggestions and choose at least one way you can downsize your life so that you can set your barn limit and give even more. If none seems to fit, come up with one of your own.
- Can you downsize your home?
- Can you sell things in your home? Would an estate sale be able to help you sell a majority of your items?
- Can you commute with only one car?
- Can you sell your new car and buy an older one?
- Can you encourage your children to leave the nest and/or begin to take responsibility for their own bills?
- Can your adult children begin paying rent? Paying utilities?
- What subscriptions can you cut?
- When was the last time you looked for cheaper options to all of your major providers (i.e., auto insurance)?

Prayer

Lord, help us to rope in our large eyes. Help us to be content with you alone. Help us to not worry about how you will supply our needs. Lord, let us remember that your track record is great. You have provided for generations before us and you have provided everything we have ever needed. No matter what happens, this year will be no different than any other. You have always supplied our needs. Let us want to grow closer to you and help us to be generous and give our tithes with a cheerful heart because everything comes from you. Amen.

CHAPTER 7

Putting Your Money
on a Mission

God is always trying to give good things to us,
but our hands are too full to receive them.

~ AUGUSTINE

Becoming part of the Giving Generation isn't just about scraping the money together to put in an offering plate. It's about cultivating a heart of gratitude and service. In order to do this, we have to find a *why* behind our giving.

At the turn of the century in 1900, there was a famous British cricket player named C. T. Studd. Not only was he popular and well-liked, but he was also wealthy. His father had passed away, leaving C. T. and his brother a large fortune, enough to never have to work again. Speaking of young, rich, and powerful—he was all three.

What did C. T. Studd do with that money, power, and youth? As a faithful Christian, devoted to seeing God's love spread across the world, he gave it away. At the age of twenty-five, he gave nearly all of his inheritance away to evangelism-focused charities. He used his fame as a cricket player to gather support for missionary efforts.

He went even further.

It's said he walked by a sign reading "Cannibals Want Missionaries." Curious, and a little confused, he walked into the presentation. The presenters were pitching an opportunity to spread the gospel, and they were firm and realistic about the cost. Their message was:

Making yourself happy is not enough of a reason to live.

"You might die for your faith."

C. T. thought to himself, *I'm willing to do that.* Inspired by D. L. Moody (another famous evangelist) and Hudson Taylor, a British missionary to China, Studd decided to become a missionary. He told his family that he was dedicating his life to this cause. As if giving away his inheritance weren't enough, he then told his family that he'd be moving to China and spreading the gospel there.

His family and friends thought he had gone mad, and the road ahead of him proved to be tough: he and his wife—yes, he also convinced his missionary wife to go with him—faced disease, starvation, rejection, and death. To C. T. Studd, it was worth it. His last reported word was "hallelujah."

What would inspire someone to leave their fortune, give everything away, and risk their life? It had to be something big—bigger than themself.

How Ordinary People Become Extraordinary

This might come as a shock to you, but making yourself happy is not enough of a reason to live. When you live for yourself, you'll not only find yourself living a small life, but you'll also find yourself feeling depressed and anxious.

The way I see it, there are two ladders you can climb in life. One is God's ladder. One is the ladder to the Good Life.

C. T. Studd seemed to understand this intuitively. For most of us, it takes a little longer. If you're like me, you live for yourself and what makes you "happy" for many years before you realize you've never been so miserable. What would you want to do if you had the chance? Here are a few questions to get you thinking:

- If you could change one thing about the world, or help one person, what would you do or who would you help?
- If you didn't have the financial responsibilities you have, what would you do with your time and money?
- What problems pull at your heartstrings?
- What makes you angry? What makes you sad?
- What passions do you have?

Maybe homelessness is an issue on your heart. Maybe you care about education or about helping veterans or about helping those with special needs. Maybe you haven't even thought that far ahead. You're not sure what you would do, but you know you'd like to make an impact somehow.

I don't know you personally, but by knowing that you picked up this book, I have a lot of respect for, you have a spirit of generosity. I know, at some point in your life, you had a dream to give back. You think to yourself, *When I make it, I'll be able to help so many people.* Your wish to give back gets buried in the routines, distractions, and demands of life.

Your aspirations get buried, and you lose heart. It feels like the best you can do is to take care of yourself and your family.

My hope for you is that you dig down deep and find that dream—because it is the dream that will fuel you to take the radical action I talked about in the last chapter. There are people out there who need you, who need to hear your story. People who need the gifts that you can offer: your skills, your wisdom, your listening ear. There are people who need the financial resources you can provide.

The truth is, *you* can make an impact that no one else can. This is the great irony of the way of Jesus. Living for yourself will make you

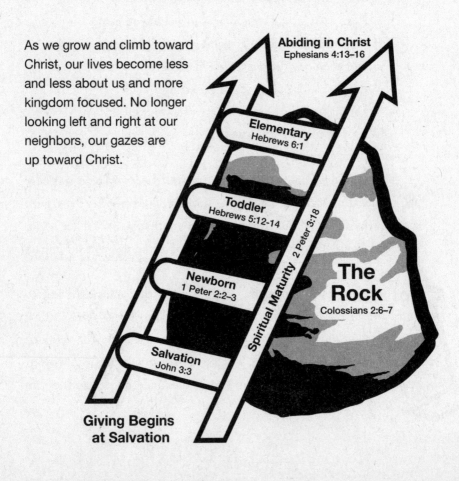

As we grow and climb toward Christ, our lives become less and less about us and more kingdom focused. No longer looking left and right at our neighbors, our gazes are up toward Christ.

Abiding in Christ
Ephesians 4:13–16

Elementary
Hebrews 6:1

Toddler
Hebrews 5:12-14

Spiritual Maturity 2 Peter 3:18

Newborn
1 Peter 2:2–3

The Rock
Colossians 2:6–7

Salvation
John 3:3

Giving Begins at Salvation

miserable. When you put your life (and your money) on a mission for Jesus, you'll find that He elevates you to tasks and positions you couldn't have ever gotten by yourself.

You are the only one who can do this.

Not all of us will be like, C. T. Studd. Not all of us will move across the globe or spend our lives spreading the Word as missionaries. But all of us can share in that purpose that C. T. had: to spread God's love, and all of us can make an impact. This, after all, is how ordinary people become extraordinary.

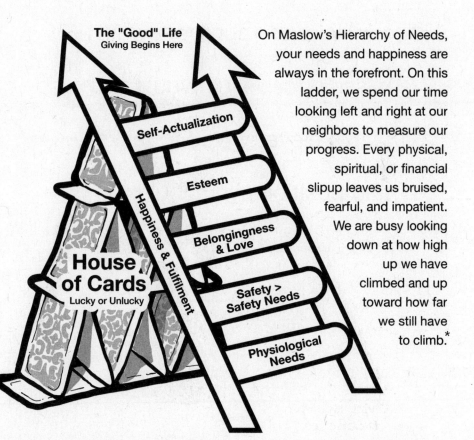

The "Good" Life
Giving Begins Here

Self-Actualization

Esteem

Belongingness & Love

Safety > Safety Needs

Physiological Needs

Happiness & Fulfillment

House of Cards
Lucky or Unlucky

On Maslow's Hierarchy of Needs, your needs and happiness are always in the forefront. On this ladder, we spend our time looking left and right at our neighbors to measure our progress. Every physical, spiritual, or financial slipup leaves us bruised, fearful, and impatient. We are busy looking down at how high up we have climbed and up toward how far we still have to climb.*

* Abraham Maslow, "A Theory of Human Motivation," *Psychological Review* 50, no. 4 (July 1943): 370–396, https://doi.org/10.1037/h0054346

———

Living for yourself will make you miserable. But when you put your life (and your money) on a mission for Jesus, you'll find that He elevates you to tasks and positions you couldn't have ever gotten by yourself.

———

Take Rob, for example. He's from my hometown of Pensacola, Florida. He is thirty-five and manages vacation rentals for a living. We met at a BCM (Baptist Collegiate Ministries) meeting one night in college. He has three kids in elementary school. When he was single, he only spent money on himself, but during premarital counseling, his then-fiancée, Melissa, said, "We must begin tithing when we get married." At that time Rob had never tithed, despite growing up in church. Since committing their finances to the Lord, Rob and Melissa have been able to give thousands of dollars to their local church and overseas missions. Their giving and involvement in local missions work even led them to become foster parents.

"If I had sat down and looked at the numbers, I would never have thought it could happen," Rob admits. "But I've learned that God's plans are different from my plans, and that God always provides a way."

Rob and Melissa had to make sacrifices: they live in a smaller house, and Melissa has started a side job to provide a little extra room in the finances. She says, "I realized that I never really needed a big house anyway. What I needed was love, and that's what I got." Together, they've changed the lives of local kids in dramatic ways, including telling the kids about Jesus, and they've funded organizations which help orphans and underprivileged children with education and resources.

How about Sarah? Sarah is a real estate agent. She's in her mid-twenties. She's always given to her local church when she could. But in the last year, she's nearly doubled her church giving every month. Not only does she find herself more involved with her community, but she is invested in the success of these ministries, and she's finding new opportunities to volunteer. She's signed up for several missions trips. Sarah has called this "the best year of my life" and her "biggest adventure yet"—all because she decided to give more.

What about David and Grace? They are fifty-five-year-olds whose kids have gone to college. As empty nesters, they weren't sure what to do with their extra time. When they started volunteering more at their local church, they became more aware of the church's financial needs. When I met with David and Grace, I asked them on a scale from 1 to 10 how important is it to leave money behind for your kids. They both looked at each other and said it's a 3. David said, "Our kids are doing better than we were at their age. We helped them with a car and getting through college, so we have done our part. Now, they're independent and we can begin giving more. We have decided not to spend our children's inheritance but to begin giving away their inheritance."

"We have decided not to spend our children's inheritance but to begin giving away their inheritance."

The couple started giving more, and doing so has provided them with new purpose and energy. You'll see them at almost every church function, welcoming new people and showing them around. They've become pillars of the church community.

When I think of my inspiration for giving, I not only think of people like C. T. Studd, I also think of people like Rob, Melissa, Sarah, David, and Grace. I think of people like my grandfather and his father before him, who gave generously even when there wasn't much to go around.

It's a lie to think that only the billionaires like Warren Buffet and Bill Gates, who donate half or 99 percent of their wealth, are making a difference. So much good can be done for our communities, for our world— and for ourselves—when we give, especially when we give beyond the 10 percent that Scripture requires.

Here's what might shock you. The more you give, the more you receive. Meaning, when you begin to give—even beyond what sometimes seems possible—you will be blessed in great measure. It's the only command-ment in the Bible where God says, "Test me in this …"

> "Test me in this … and see if I will not throw open the floodgates of heaven and pour out so much blessing that there will not be room enough to store it" (Malachi 3:10 NIV).

What if we tested God in this as He has asked us to? What could be possible if we became not only a generation of generous givers, but we also began to influence the world at large? If giving is generative like this—if we truly can't outgive God—there is no end to the needs we could meet if we began to think of our money in this way. If the 95 percent of the church that isn't tithing began to tithe, the result would be an additional $165 billion given each year. That funding could be dispersed in the following ways:

- $25 billion could relieve global hunger, starvation, and deaths from preventable diseases in five years.
- $12 billion could eliminate illiteracy in five years.
- $15 billion could solve the world's water and sanitation issues, specifically in places where 1 billion people live on less than $1 per day.
- $1 billion could fully fund all overseas mission work and help evangelize the 6,600 unreached people groups across the globe that don't even know who Jesus is.[23]

This is what's possible when we stop thinking of our money as "ours" and start putting it on a mission for Jesus.

Money on a Mission

I want to go back for a minute to this mistaken idea we sometimes have that money is the root of all evil. The phrase comes from a Bible verse, but here's the catch: it's often misquoted. Actually, 1 Timothy 6:10 says, "For the *love* of money is *a root of all kinds* of evils. It is through this *craving* that some have wandered away from the faith and pierced themselves with many pangs" (emphasis mine).

Money is not evil, but it provides an opportunity for evil. What this passage is getting at here is that money can *either* be a gateway to heaven or a gateway to hell. We are at a crossroads. We get to choose. All of this hangs on what we do with our money. Do we see it as "ours"? Or do we see it as a tool we get to use for the kingdom?

Notice that word again: *craving*. It's the endless craving, chasing, desiring that gets in our way. When money becomes our endgame, we start using people to get money. We abuse power to grow personal wealth. We've seen this in history, we've seen this in our personal lives, and maybe we can even admit that we've done this, ourselves. We know where that craving leads: only to more craving.

The reason the craving never ends isn't a problem with money itself. It has to do with our approach to money. It's that we're throwing money at the wrong things. The truth is, you are not a big enough reason to live for. We are not made to live strictly for ourselves. The craving will never stop until we find purpose in something worthy of our time, energy, and money—something worth living and even dying for.

My goal is not to make you feel guilty about your wealth. Quite the opposite: I believe you should be a hard worker and prosperous because you bring so much value to your community that people cannot wait to hand over their money to you. I hope you make *as much money as possible*, and I hope you can give it away too.

If you're confused about where or how to give, think about the early church in Acts (from the last chapter I shared with you) and ask yourself what needs are right in front of you, in your immediate community.

+ Who is hungry and needs a meal?
+ Who is hurting and needs some comfort?
+ Who is carrying a heavy burden and could use some support?
+ Who has a need they can't meet on their own?
+ Who might benefit from something you have to give away?

The Holy Spirit showed the church in Acts how to take care of one another, so too will He show you. The beautiful thing is, the power and importance of the gospel hasn't waned. The gospel is as worthy to give to as it was 2,000 years ago.

The gospel is what transforms people. God's love is what makes a lasting and eternal difference. The truth is what sets people free.

Servanthood Index

The creation of the scoring rubric for this assessment took an in-depth scripture study of Matthew 25:40–45 and 1 Corinthians 12:21–27. Every believer has a significant role to play in the church and the spread of the gospel. It is between the believer and God's plan what your role will be. My humble belief is that as followers, we must desire and strive to practice the following spiritual disciplines for each of these people groups.

When answering each question, you can count your fruit using the following scoring (see Luke 13:6–9):

0 - None Praying - 1 Giving - 2 Serving - 3 Praying, Giving and Serving - 4

What has been your involvement in serving each of the following?

_____ **Orphans or children in need of adoption or foster care**
(Psalm 82:3) Organization Example: Florida Baptist Children's Homes

_____ **Christians in financial need**
(James 2:15–17) Organization Example: LifeWater International

_____ **Immigrants**
(Deuteronomy 10:19, Matthew 25:35) Organization Example: Samaritan's Purse

_____ **Single or expectant mothers**
(Psalm 139:13–18) Organization Example: Bethany Christian Services

_____ **Unreached people groups in this country**
(Romans 10:14–21) Organization Example: Urgent

_____ **Prisoners**
(Matthew 25:34–40) Organization Example: Bill Glass Behind the Walls

_____ **Missionaries**
Philippians 4:16–18) Organization Example: International Mission Board (IMB)

____ **Your local church**
(Mark 12:17) Organization Example:
A biblically based local church

____ **Expanding access and translations of the Bible**
(Matthew 28:19–20) Organization Example: Gideons

____ **Those affected by natural disasters**
(James 2:15–17) Organization Example:
Florida Baptist Convention Disaster Relief

____ **Widows – The elderly who are on limited
fixed income**
(James 1:27) Organization Example:
The Ministries of Heaven's Family

____ **People preparing for vocational ministry
(seminary/Bible schools)**
(Psalm 119:9) Organization Example: Word of Life

____ **People with disabilities**
(Luke 14:12–14) Organization Example:
Night to Shine (Tim Tebow Foundation)

____ **The poor or homeless**
(Matthew 6:1–4, Luke 3:11) Organization
Example: Compassion International

____ **People who lack adequate health care**
(Acts 20:35) Organization Example:
Christian Health Service Corps

____ **People who are malnourished or food insecure**
(Isaiah 58:7–10, Proverbs 22:9) Organization
Example: Manna Food Bank

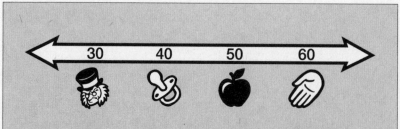

 Good & Faithful Servant (Matthew 25:21). Score: 50 to 64. There are no greater words we can hope to hear from our Father in heaven when we meet Him face-to-face. As you continue to serve God by serving others, please remember Matthew 6:1: "Beware of practicing your righteousness before other people in order to be seen by them, for then you will have no reward from your Father who is in heaven." Even despite your high score on this assessment, I hope there were people groups you felt convicted to serve at a deeper level.

 Elementary (Hebrews 6:1–20). Score: 35 to 40. You may want to spend some of your quiet time asking the Lord to help open more opportunities for you to serve. After the assessment, I hope you are encouraged to begin giving monetarily to a group, in addition to praying for them. If you are already giving, maybe you could begin serving the group as well.

 Infancy (Hebrews 5:12–14). Score: 20 to 35. Do not beat yourself up too hard. The assessment is designed to encourage you to get involved with more of these people groups. Our hope is that the Holy Spirit revealed to you multiple needs of your neighbors and opportunities that help generate future gospel conversations.

 Ebeneezer Scrooge (Philippians 1:6). Score: 0 to 20. First off, don't question your salvation or anything silly like that. My prayer is the Holy Spirit will warm your heart to those people groups you have overlooked that are afflicted and in need of the gospel. You may need to calibrate your calendar and check your checking account to grow in maturity with your walk with Christ. Pray for ongoing conviction to pray often, give generously, and seek to serve those who are in great need.

As Christians, we will be salt and light when we show love to those who are hurting (John 13:34–45). We should have a heart for all of these people. Remember Jesus' words in Matthew 7:21: "Not everyone who says to me, 'Lord, Lord,' will enter the kingdom of heaven, but the one who does the will of my Father who is in heaven." We should be found busy serving toward His will.

By contributing toward our churches and toward Christian ministries, we spread the gospel. We *get* to use money to win hearts for Christ.

When used for kingdom purposes, to spread God's love, money can do a lot of good, and it can empower us to make a big impact.

A Mission Worth Living For

Think of the last time you felt a strong sense of purpose in the world something running deep through your bones. Have you ever felt grateful to merely get to *serve*? This is what it feels like to have not only a cause worth dying for, like C. T. Studd, but a mission worth living for.

Most assessments are about either how you see the world or how the world sees you. However, what will matter at the end of your life is not how the world sees you nor how you see the world, but how God sees you.

How can we expand our reach in order to expand our hearts?

Disclaimer:

We know that works do not equate to salvation. We understand that works are an outpouring result of salvation. Salvation is the seed and the fruit are your works. As believers, we take great comfort in understanding that no amount of service, giving, good deeds, and gospel conversations can increase Christ's love for each of us. The previous assessment is not to give you a pat on the back or defeat you. The assessment serves to encourage you on your stewardship journey. The index has been designed with the use of these supporting scriptures.

If you look back over your life, I think you'll find that it's the moments of *service* that bring us out of ourselves. They remind us that our comfort or amusement is not the most important part of life. These moments grow our character and transform us into someone who reflects Jesus' love in a way that moments of ease or temporary "happiness" never could.

Examples would be: getting your hands dirty while serving in a disaster relief ministry. Laughing and crying alongside young mothers while counseling them through an unexpected pregnancy. Playing catch with a foster child while raising them to know the Lord. Drinking tea with an elderly woman after leading a Bible study at an assisted living community.

That's what purpose feels like.

We want to make a difference, but we're only thinking about ourselves and our families. How can we expand our reach in order to expand our hearts?

When we finally let go of the need to accumulate for ourselves, a whole world of possibility opens up. There's a liberation in becoming part of a cause bigger than yourself.

The sky's the limit. You can do anything with your life if you follow God's guidance. Then the kind of impact you can have—and the abundant life you will enjoy—is endless.

Chapter 7: Reader's Guide

Biblical Text to Study: Ecclesiastes 2:4–8 and
Ecclesiastes 5:10–20

Discussion	• How did you score on the servanthood index? • How can you switch from climbing the culture's ladder to climbing God's ladder of success in your life?
Framework	**The Two Ladders Illustration** Go back to the Two Ladders illustration and ask yourself which ladder you have been climbing. What would it look like to get off of culture's ladder and onto God's?
Memorization	**Ecclesiastes 3:10–11** *I have seen the business that God has given to the children of man to be busy with. He has made everything beautiful in its time. Also, he has put eternity into man's heart.*
Group Leader Questions:	• Is it sobering that there is nothing we can do in our lifetime that hasn't really already been done? You are only improving and creating a new way of doing things that have already been done under the sun. • Why do we still waste our time testing what Solomon has already proved? • Why does success leave us yearning for more? • Everyone has eternity in their heart. How can we build upon that in gospel conversations? • How do these verses connect with 1 Timothy 6:6–10?

Action Item

Complete the servanthood index from this chapter. Then sit down with an accountability partner who will help hold you accountable on taking actionable steps toward practicing these disciplines for others. Better yet, be brave enough to share your results with your connect group or Bible study group. Encourage your whole class to take it. If you can, get your class involved so that as a group, all of you can began integrating more service and gospel conversation opportunities into your schedule of events.

Prayer

Lord, give me wisdom like you entrusted to Solomon to help me live a life of value, not vanity. Help me to speak the truth of the gospel in a way for unbelieving hearts to hear. Let me never forget to shout of your good deeds and wear my thankfulness for your provision. Correct my ways from seeking fulfillment in my passions and pursuits. Lead me to always seek your will first. Aid me to build my life on your rock, for this is a sturdy foundation indeed. Amen.

CHAPTER 8

Testing Your Treasure

The only things we can keep
are the things we freely give to God.
~ C. S. LEWIS

One year my wife, Natasha, and I vacationed in Savannah, Georgia. When we arrived, before we even settled in, we spent the day taking in the beautiful city covered in old live oaks. We stopped at a coffee shop, then wandered into a boutique, where we found a few paintings that we fell in love with. Since we were still decorating our place back home in Pensacola, we decided to buy them.

The shopping continued across the street at another boutique, where we found a wooden buffet table that would be perfect for our livingroom. We got lost in the hunt and soon loaded up our truck with several more pieces for home. By the end of the day, we were exhausted and ready to finally see our accommodations for the night, a room in a majestic Victorian home turned into a hotel.

It was late, so we followed the self check-in instructions quickly and headed to our room, but we were in for a surprise. When we opened the door, we found the place empty: No bed. No couch. No furniture of any kind. No decorations on the walls. Not at all what we had expected from the advertisement.

There had obviously been a mistake: this room was in the midst of a renovation. As I called the host to set up new accommodations, Natasha tried to make light of the situation, saying, "At least we bought all this furniture today! We can bring it up and make the place our own!"

She was, of course, kidding. Why would we decorate a hotel room with our own furniture and art? We were only planning on being there for a short period of time, but what she said resonated with me on a spiritual level. I had an epiphany that stopped me in my tracks. It was as if God was asking me, "Where is your true home, Andrew? You know this life is only temporary. Why are you so focused on how it looks?"

No one would spend everything they had to decorate a hotel room. It's not our permanent home. Spiritually, our permanent home is heaven. Why would I invest in what is temporary when I could invest in something which lasts forever?

The Only Thing We Take with Us

Sadly, most of what we accumulate will waste away in a handful of years or in less than one hundred and fifty years in a landfill. Even our most sacred heirlooms will ultimately find themselves in strangers' hands within a few generations, where they will be abused and mistreated. Most of what we spend our money on doesn't last for our lifetime and certainly not for eternity.

We don't get to take everything with us.

Not only do these things fail to last for eternity—the feelings they give fail to last more than a few days. How often does what we buy seem immediately less valuable once it's in our possession? This is the kind of happiness which leaves as the new car smell fades or once someone else has what you have. Experiences can be the same way, leaving you increasingly emptier than you wished. It's the kind of high that leaves you low.

By contrast, some of our work, experience, and things truly stay with us; they motivate us onward, even when times are tough. They make us say, "It was all worth it." The Gospel of Matthew says, "Do not lay up for yourselves treasures on earth, where moth and rust destroy and where thieves break in and steal, but lay up for yourselves treasures in heaven, where neither moth nor rust destroys and where thieves do not break in and steal. For where your treasure is, there your heart will be also" (Matthew 6:19–21). The treasure of our time, resources, and energy need to be invested in what is of God if it is to last. This is the only treasure which we take with us.

If we're going to create lives of lasting meaning and impact, we have to get really good at identifying what's actually going to last—what's temporary, and what's for our forever home with God.

Finding What Lasts: A Spiritual Refinery

As we get closer and closer to God, we are better able to see what has lasting power and what doesn't, what is heavenly treasure and what isn't, what is of God and what isn't. The New Testament gives us vivid imagery for this process: a fiery refinery. A refinery purifies a substance. Using fire to refine metals is one of the oldest methods of refining. When heated to a melting point, what is not pure can be separated from the metal. What's left is pure, one substance. The apostle Paul compared this process to our spiritual lives:

———

The treasure of our time,

resources, and energy need

to be invested in what is

of God if it is to last.

———

According to the grace of God given to me, like a skilled master builder I laid a foundation, and someone else is building upon it. Let each one take care how he builds upon it. For no one can lay a foundation other than that which is laid, which is Jesus Christ. Now if anyone builds on the foundation with gold, silver, precious stones, wood, hay, straw—each one's work will become manifest, for the Day will disclose it, because it will be revealed by fire, and the fire will test what sort of work each one has done. If the work that anyone has built on the foundation survives, he will receive a reward. If anyone's work is burned up, he will suffer loss, though he himself will be saved, but only as through fire. (1 Corinthians 3:10–15)

Spiritually, a refinery burns away anything that is not of God. What doesn't burn away is what's eternally valuable. The refinery takes you through the layers of heat, which peel away the material things until you reach what will last forever. If it doesn't burn up, you have something of value.

This is not the first time the Scriptures use the metaphor of a refinery. In the Old Testament book of Malachi, the prophet of the Lord addressed the people of Israel, speaking of a messenger who would come to set right the relationship between Yahweh and the people, partly through reform, or purification, of the religious leaders:[24]

But who can endure the day of his coming, and who can stand when he appears? For he is like a refiner's fire and like fullers' soap. He will sit as a refiner and purifier of silver, and he will purify the sons of Levi and refine them like gold and silver, and they will bring offerings in righteousness to the LORD (Malachi 3:2–3).

Distinguishing between what is of God and what is not is a biblical theme that surfaces again and again.

The theme remains relevant today. Our lives, too, are a mix. What we invest in and what we put money toward is a mix. Do our investments matter in an *eternal* kind of way, or are they less significant than that?

The color of a fire is a clear sign of how hot the fire really is. The yellow flame of the fire is approximately 2,000 kelvin, while the red flame measures about 3,000 kelvin, and the blue flame (the hottest flame) is north of 5,000 kelvin. Take a minute to think about the assets you have accumulated over a lifetime and ask: How many of them would stand the heat of the fire?

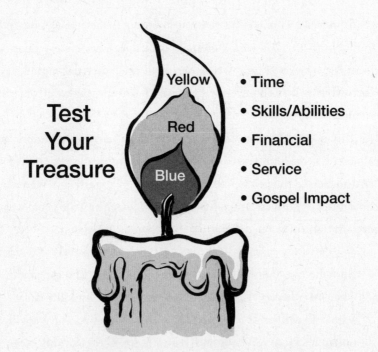

Use the above imagery to "swap" your earthly
treasure for something much more lasting.

The first step toward creating a life of spiritual gold—a life which will lead to lasting fulfillment—is to test the treasure you have now, to examine your life. What I've learned is that there are essentially three steps to putting your life through this kind of spiritual refinery.

Step 1: Identify the Treasure

The first step in testing your treasure is to identify it. Another way of asking, "What is your treasure?" is to ask, "What do you value?" As the Gospel of Matthew says, your treasure reveals your *heart*.

There are some values which we're proud to name as treasures: family, faith, work. If pressed further, we might say that we value our country, our kids' education, or the light of Jesus spread in the world. But, for most of us, there's another list of things we don't *realize* we value, which actually take up a lot of our time, money, and effort: our image, our social standing, and our status, to name a few.

What we *invest in* shows what we value. We could spend an entire day listing out all the different pieces of our lives we value. Fortunately, there are two indicators which reflect your most valued treasure right away: your bank account and your calendar. Show me your calendar and bank records or credit card statement, and I can tell you where your heart is also.

Your checking account and your calendar are like contrast dye. Contrast dye is the substance that helps radiologists diagnose medical conditions. Contrast dye injected intravenously will illuminate cancers and diseases which may not show up in an MRI scan. The dye runs through the patient's blood system and groups within the infectious area.

Time and money act similarly in your life. Our checking accounts and calendars reveal what we truly value and in turn expose our loyalties. For example, if your checking account showed a purchase of an Alabama football jersey, Alabama football tickets, and other Alabama merchandise, I could reasonably guess that you're an Alabama fan. If your calendar has dates blocked off for Alabama games, then my reasonable guess would be confirmed: you're a true Alabama fan.[25]

Your passion and joy usually sit right between your time and your money. When I started courting Natasha, my wife, I spent money on her as often as I could. I sent her roses, bought her gifts, and took her on unique dates. I spent as much time as possible with her, texting her, taking her out, and then calling her later. I wanted to show her that I was invested in our relationship. Where you spend your time and money says more about your treasure than almost anything else.

Ask yourself where your money is going. At this point in the book, you've likely already had some time to reflect on this. In this case, I want you to go through at least one month's bank statements—line by line. Where is your money allocated? I challenge you to journal your expenses for a week. It might feel trivial (and it is a lot of work), but you will also be amazed at what you find. Seemingly small expenses add up quickly. Where do the largest dollar amounts go in a week? How about in a month? Where is your "treasure"? In America, we eat out nearly 50 percent of our meals, which accounts for 5.1 percent of the average consumer's income. Many of these meals out we are having are out of convenience. It all adds up extremely quickly and, after getting accustomed to this routine, we can find ourselves asking, "Where is all of our money going?"

You may have heard it said that money changes people, that when someone acquires more money, they become a different person. I disagree. Money is an indicator; it's that contrast dye. It flows to what matters to us. More money simply makes it easier for outsiders to identify what a person had always valued in the first place.

Time is the same way. In fact, you could do a similar activity with your calendar. Look at a month's worth of activities on your calendar and ask yourself: *Where is my time going?* Likely, many of your weekly hours go toward work and, if you have kids, family life. Where else does the rest of your time go?

What do you value enough to spend time doing?

Step 2: Stoke the Fire

Once you have a list of your "treasure," it's time to see what will make it through God's refinery. It's not always easy to identify what has spiritual weight and what doesn't, but here are a few characteristics of what might burn away.

Yellow Flame – Pass your treasures through this first sifting test. These treasures often melt quickly and show their true colors under high heat. Most of these don't even pass the secular test of prudent money management. These expenditures are often not gems but whims. They are pursuits that have a likelihood of changing next week. I may be willing to give my excess spare change to them, but nothing more. I believe the following expenses meet the needs of my family, myself, and maybe others, but with no real kingdom impact.

Characteristics of spending on these "treasures:"

- Leave you feeling empty
- Immediately depreciates in value
- Has no return on investment
- Easily replaceable
- Things you often don't pray about
- Distracts you from what you actually care about in your life
- Short-lived feeling of security
- Encourages a feeling of inferiority among others

Examples:
- Cars
- Games
- Entertainment
- Electronics
- Furniture
- Clothing

Red Flame – Next, pass your treasures through these purifying flames. These are treasures that the world would gasp at because they are considered investments. They refer to them as assets, not like the liabilities of the yellow-flame test. Let us be careful, though; *one man's preparation for the future* is *another's idol*, but with God, all is but a vapor. However, these treasures can and should be used to leverage toward furthering the gospel, discipleship, refuge, and a place to foster those in need of help. However, often they are not utilized for gospel ministry but to minister to our own comfort.

Characteristics of spending on these treasures:
- Leave you feeling self-made
- Appreciate in value
- Has a return on investment
- Expensive to replace
- Things you often pray for more of
- Can distract you by becoming all you care about
- Long-lived feeling of misplaced security
- Encourages a feeling of superiority over others

Examples:
- Homes
- Investments

+ Collectibles
+ Education

Blue Flame – Lastly, pass your treasures through this cleansing test. These are treasures that help fund ministries. These you are willing to spend your life pursuing. This list is not only worth living for but worth dying for if necessary. I believe strongly that these meet the needs of others, but more importantly, these treasures help to advance the gospel to others.

Characteristics of spending on these treasures:
+ Leave you feeling full of gratitude
+ Exponential in value
+ Unquantifiable return on investment
+ Irreplacable—no replacement ever needed
+ Things that help you pray more often
+ Refocuses on what God cares about
+ Peace that surpasses circumstances and understanding
+ Encourages a feeling of compassion for others

Examples:
+ Physical Donations
+ Tithing
+ Offerings
+ Volunteering

Alternatively, what lasts has opposite effects:
+ Gives you a sense of purpose in the world
+ Utilizes your spiritual gifts
+ Spreads God's love
+ Helps others tangibly

+ Teaches about Jesus
+ Feeds your soul
+ Calms your anxious thoughts
+ Is something you want to treasure for a long time
+ Helps you feel connected to others

After going through the above lists, you might already be getting an idea of what needs to stay and what needs to go in your life. Below are a few questions to ask yourself that will help you continue to separate the gold (which lasts) from what doesn't:

+ What is it providing to others?
+ Am I learning and growing from this?
+ Am I willing to volunteer my time?
+ Does this demonstrate God's love?
+ Is this something which, ultimately, wins people for Christ?

Now that you're starting to wrap your head around what might need to be cut from your life, you're probably asking: What about normal tasks and responsibilities which don't seem to align with kingdom purposes? For example, going to the dentist. That has to be done, but is it deeply meaningful to you? Not so much.

I'm not asking you to quit your job, stop socializing, and only go to church and volunteer every day. There are plenty of things you do in your life not because they are ministries but because they are totally necessary for our normal lives: clothes, a home, food, medicine, etc. (As a side note, think about how your time at the dentist *could* become a ministry with the right mindset!)

We don't carry anything physical into the next life. But what is spiritual lasts. That doesn't mean your house is useless or that you can never buy nice things. It means that you need to ask yourself a question: *Does my investment have spiritual weight? How many spiritual carats are in this investment?*

A friend of mine bought a new home, and, having us over one night, he confessed how guilty he felt about it. I sat him down and said, "Jerod, look at what you're doing with your home: you're raising your kids, you are hosting a Bible study, you are taking care of neighbors and relatives. You are using your home for good."

To be honest, I'm not worried about Jerod. I know his heart, and his house is not something he bought to show off or to make himself look better. What concerns me more is the mindless spending we all do: when we invest without considering if what we're spending our time or money on is actually giving us the kind of life and purpose that we actually want. We want a life of purpose—and the chase never satisfies.

Step 3: Trade Your Earthly Treasure for what Counts

In the early 1800s my great-great-grandfather Daniel McNair left Scotland, fleeing from the devastation brought on by the highland potato famine. He left for a better life: consistent income, regular meals, and the hope that he'd strike it rich in America.

As he prepared to leave his country, Scottish money became less and less useful to him. He sold everything he could and traded his money in for American dollars. It would have been a waste for him to continue investing in his Scottish home. He knew he was leaving; he only kept enough to sustain him as he prepared for a better future.

As believers, we can be confident that this earth is not our permanent home. The book of Philippians describes our belonging to a future home as citizenship: "But our citizenship is in heaven, and from it we await a Savior, the Lord Jesus Christ" (Philippians 3:20). The book of Hebrews says, "For here we have no lasting city, but we seek the city that is to come" (Hebrews 13:14).

If you find that your life is not full of much treasure that lasts, it's time to exchange the temporary for the eternal. Maybe it's clear to you how you could increase that treasure, but maybe you're new to a giving practice, and you're not sure where to start. That's a normal feeling, and it can be overwhelming, as there are many organizations that need our finances and our volunteer efforts.

With all of that in mind, here's what you need to know: God has a specific call on your life. How do I know? Because God has a specific call on *all* lives. What you are called to do and where you are called to give depends a lot on your experience and on how God made you.

Ask the Lord to use His winnowing fork in your life. As we see in Matthew 3:12, "His winnowing fork is in his hand, and he will clear his threshing floor and gather his wheat into the barn, but the chaff he will burn with unquenchable fire." What the Lord has promised to do at the end of the age is what He will do for you at any age of your life. He will help you go through your spending and separate out the chaff. It's time to repent and ask the Holy Spirit to do a work in your finances.

How you spend your money is a smoldering to your neighbors and ultimately to Christ. 2 Corinthians 2:15 tells us, "For we are the aroma of Christ to God among those who are being saved and among those who are perishing." Do not waste your life and finances on things that will not bring a sweet aroma to the Lord. Spend some time thinking and reflecting on the following questions:

+ What makes you righteously angry?
+ What makes you smile with joy?
+ What does a successful Christian life look like to you?
+ What stories leave you with happy tears?
+ What is your testimony? How did Christ transform your life?
+ Who were you before you met Christ? Who do you think you would have become without Christ? Remember this famous

saying: You are most qualified to help the person you were or who you would have become.

+ What organizations are you already involved with? Are there other ministries you are passionate about?

These are indicators of where you should be giving and about what God's will is for your life. What can you trade in?

Ask yourself:

+ Can I cut down on discretionary spending?
+ What takes a lot of my time and money which isn't adding much to my life?
+ What is actually leading me further away from God?
+ What can I do to reduce expenses or gain a little extra income?

Revelation 3:18 says, "I counsel you to buy from me gold refined by fire, so that you may be rich. ..." In this passage, we are challenged to trade our present possessions for eternal gold. Trade your earthly riches for permanent everlasting riches, like selling or reducing your earthly possessions for a greater purpose.

Paradox of Christianity

Immediately prior to the story of the Rich Young Ruler in Matthew, we read the story of Jesus and the little children (Matthew 19:13–15). The wisdom of the world would tell a leader like Jesus to focus on the followers who could lend His teachings social credibility: the rich and influential people. Jesus did the opposite: He spent time with those without any status, influence, or money. He valued children—the least of these.

Christianity is full of paradoxes. Jesus said, "Blessed are the poor" (Luke 6:20). He said, "The last will be first, and the first last" (Matthew 20:16). Taking a more hard-hitting stance, Jesus said, "But woe to you

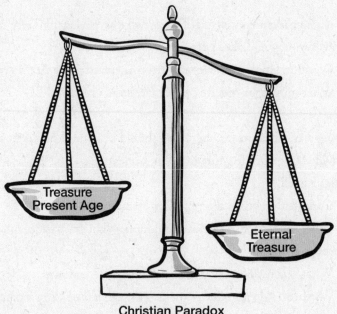

Christian Paradox

who are rich, for you have received your consolation. Woe to you who are full now, for you shall be hungry" (Luke 6:24–25).

If you say, "I am rich," Christ says you are poor. If you say, "I am wealthy," Christ says you are empty. You may say, "I have everything," but Christ says, "You have nothing that truly matters." When we're not willing to help those around us, when we are unwilling to extend generosity to the poor, we find that the true poverty is within us. We are not cultivating treasure which lasts.

When we are unwilling to extend generosity to the poor, we find that the true poverty is *within* us.

What's clear is that the success, status, wealth, and possessions we accumulate here—our riches and power—do not impress God, and, ultimately, they do not fulfill us. We are made in God's image and, as much as we think money, wealth, and power will fulfill us, we were made for more.

If we're going to follow God's way of creating lasting fulfillment in our lives, we're going to have to start investing in something else: something that lasts.

Chapter 8: Reader's Guide

Biblical Text to Study: Matthew 6:19–21

Discussion	• What are the things you treasure most in your life? • Using the refinery analogy, what treasures did you find were yellow, red, or blue? • Is anyone brave enough to share some items in their home or in their life that won't make it through the refinery?
Framework	**Test Your Treasure** If you haven't already, go back to the "test your treasure" illustration in this chapter and ask yourself if what you value will make it into the kingdom of heaven.
Memorization	**Matthew 6:21** *"For where your treasure is, there your heart will be also."*
Group Leader Questions	• Is anyone brave enough to share some items in their home or in your life that won't make it through the refinery? • In your own life, how have you witnessed time's stealthy breakdown on health and wealth? • Have you ever mistaken a prosperous time in your life for God's favor? Can God teach us anything in a bankruptcy or backslide financially? • How do you think Matthew 13:44 parallels with Matthew 6:19-21?

Action item   Journal your expenses for one week. After the week, analyze with your spouse or an accountability partner what could be eliminated.

Prayer   Lord, in your words to the prophet Jeremiah (17:9–10) you said, "The heart is deceitful above all things, and desperately wicked; who can know it? I, the LORD, search the heart, I test the mind, even to give every man according to his ways, according to the fruit of his doings" (NKJV). I pray earnestly that you keep our hearts pure and untainted so that we can have a cheerful and generous heart toward the things you value, for they have eternal ramifications. Help us to center our hearts on the things you value, helping us to avoid getting caught in the mundane activities of today and overlooking the lost, the downtrodden, and those you want us to minister to. Help us to see the reflection of our hearts and how bankrupt we would be without you within us. You promised that you would change our hearts by placing your Holy Spirit within us and changing us from the inside out. I pray that you continue your work within my heart to change me. In your matchless name, Amen.

CHAPTER 9

Creating an Eternal Inheritance

Oh, my dear Christians! If you would be like Christ,
give much, give often, give freely, to the vile and the poor,
the thankless and the undeserving. Christ is glorious
and happy, and so will you be. It is not your money
I want, but your happiness. Remember his own
Word: It is more blessed to give than to receive.

~ R. M. MCCHEYNE

I t seems like everyone wants to make more money. Yet they're not sure why. When I challenge people on why they are so concerned with making and keeping money, the conversation usually goes something like this:

Me: Why do you want to make more money?

You: So I can have a better life, buy a nicer house, and have the things I want.

Me: Once you have those things, then what?

You: I'll travel, explore the world, and do things I always wanted to do.

Me: After you have traveled the world and mastered your hobbies, then what?

You: I'll have freedom to relax and enjoy leisure living.

Me: Then what?

You: Then I'll leave my kids and their kids an inheritance.

That's what it all comes down to: our comfort, our leisure, and, last of all, leaving an inheritance for our grandkids. We all know that we can't take our treasure with us when we die, so the next best thing to do with our money, we believe, is to give it to our kids, to leave it for posterity.

This comes from a good place: We love our children. We love our grandchildren. We want to make a way for them. We don't want them to struggle, and we want the best life possible for them, lives better than our own lives. We want them to appreciate the love we have for them. We want them to succeed, and we feel joy when we're the ones who are able to help them. It makes sense that, at the end of our lives, we would leave them as much money as possible, right?

Maybe.

The Problem of Passing on Money

Proverbs praises those who leave an inheritance for their children: "A good man leaves an inheritance to his children's children, but the sinner's wealth is laid up for the righteous" (Proverbs 13:22). I agree with this. Giving is an act of generosity. Giving to our children is one sign that we are living godly lives. What I want to challenge is the idea that giving money to our children is the most *valuable* inheritance that you can give them. Is more money actually what your kids and grandkids want?

I have settled the accounts of many deceased clients. That process involves sitting down with their children and grandchildren. Not a single time have I found a family anxious to get their hands on property or wealth. What do those children and grandchildren want? They want more of the person they lost. They want to hear their stories again—how they met their spouse or where they were when they heard the news about JFK. They want more time to ask about how it was back then, or about how and why they immigrated here to America. They want their advice, encouragement, and support. They want someone's hand to hold when they're not sure they can handle life's challenges.

As those who are departing, it's tempting to think that leaving our kids money might soften the pain or fill the void. Money cannot fill this void. Your kids are wise: they'll know if you're trying to make up for something with money.

"I didn't want his money," I've heard people say. "I wanted more of my dad." Money isn't only *not* what our kids want from us, it also doesn't necessarily help them become better people. I've seen frugal grandparents pass on everything they worked so hard for, only to see their children's children spend it quickly and thoughtlessly.

Andrew Carnegie called this out when he wrote, "The almighty dollar bequeathed to a child is an almighty curse. The thoughtful man must admit to himself that it is not the welfare of the children but family pride which inspired these enormous legacies."[26] Carnegie's point bears reflecting.

Are we doing this for the children or for family pride?

You worked hard for your money. Spending the last decade of my life with retirees, I know this to be true: you spent years gathering the wealth your family enjoys now. While you're happy to provide a better life for your kids, you know that they will never quite appreciate what you earned because you can't quite appreciate something you yourself didn't work for. Your grandkids are even further removed from your frugal parents. It's not necessarily that your family is ungrateful; they just don't have the same experience that you do.

You might wonder, silently, if leaving your wealth to your family might hurt family relationships more than it helps them. But you're not sure what else to do. Might I suggest to you: let's explore what's possible for you *and* your family, while you're still here. Let's explore that you might not have to leave all of your wealth behind.

Perhaps you could learn about generosity as a family. Perhaps you could all leave an Eternal Legacy—*together.*

A New Kind of Inheritance

What if, instead of passing on a legacy of family pride, you passed on a legacy of generosity? God leaves us, His children, an inheritance. That inheritance is not money. It is not earthly. It is heavenly. The apostle Peter says:

> Blessed be the God and Father of our Lord Jesus Christ! According to his great mercy, he has caused us to be born again to a living hope through the resurrection of Jesus Christ from the dead, to an inheritance that is imperishable, undefiled, and unfading, kept in heaven for you, who by God's power are being guarded through faith for a salvation ready to be revealed in the last time (1 Peter 1:3–5).

If God's good gifts to His children are heavenly, couldn't our good gifts toward our children be eternal as well? We can't give our children salvation; only Jesus can do that. We can teach them how to give, how to invest in eternal treasure, and how to create lives of purpose.

Don't worry about leaving your millions to your grandkids. As the illustration goes, don't give them fish—teach them how to fish. Give them wisdom. Pass on values. Show them how to win souls for Christ and share God's love. Whether you're a grandparent, parent, or adult role model of any kind, there are plenty of easy, actionable ways to do this.

Passing on Generosity

What are your earliest memories of money? My guess is that they might have to do with your parents—or with some kind of savings bank you kept in your closet.

What will your kids' memories with money be? If your kids are already grown, how about your grandchildren? There is plenty of opportunity there for you to have an influence.

I believe that the best way to learn generosity is through your family. I know that I was only able to become generous through the example of my family. My grandfather was a generous man. He talked about how important generosity was to him. My parents were generous people. Their lives had ripple effects.

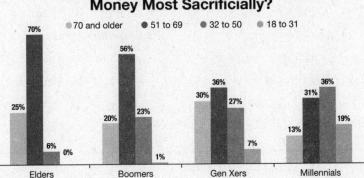

Which Generation in Your Church Gives Money Most Sacrificially?

70 and older • 51 to 69 • 32 to 50 • 18 to 31

Elders: 25%, 70%, 6%, 0%
Boomers: 20%, 56%, 23%, 1%
Gen Xers: 30%, 36%, 27%, 7%
Millennials: 13%, 31%, 36%, 19%

———

We can't give our children salvation; only Jesus can do that. We can teach them how to give, how to invest in eternal treasure, and how to create lives of purpose.

———

We must not rely on the church alone to teach our families about biblical stewardship. It's our duty to try—to teach our kids how to save and how to give, regardless of the result. The truth is, some may adopt your frugality and generosity, and others might not. But kids are extremely impressionable. As you can see below, the grandparents and parents who valued and practiced generosity produced generous children. Instructing your grandchildren, children, and those you are discipling does not have to be elaborate

We can teach our children the way to give and how to develop a generous heart. David Green, founder of Hobby Lobby, is someone who does this well. Hobby Lobby gives 50 percent of its profits away. Green brings his whole family into the decision-making process: where to give that money. Unlike many rich families of yesterday who counted their wealth and planned their businesses' world domination, the Green family abandoned the notion of the rich getting richer. Instead, they are helping the spiritual poor find riches. They are leveraging their business success for the kingdom.

You might be thinking to yourself, *I'm nowhere close to being able to leave millions to my kids—or to any ministry for that matter!* That's totally okay, and I don't expect you to have millions of dollars left over at the end of your life. But the lessons still apply: it's always better to teach a child *how to fish*. Become an example of generosity in your family, and you will *show* your kids what matters most in life.

Where you put your money speaks loudly.

You don't have to do this with millions of dollars. I bribed my nephews with $100 bills. I asked them to read *Rich Dad, Poor Dad*. Upon completion, I paid them the money. If you're giving an allowance to your kids, I suggest being hands-on with your money. Set up a tithing piggy bank. Explain the importance of giving, and the primary importance of giving to God what is already God's. When

Sunday comes around, teach them these habits of giving into the offering plate.

Set up another bank for saving. Choose, together, something for them to be saving for. Determine how much they need to save by the end of the year. This teaches them delayed gratification—something that many adults have not yet mastered! The final bucket is for spending money on whatever they want.

Gratitude is best learned hands-on. For example, one of my close friends, together with his family, selects a charity to focus on once a year. As a family, they give financially to this charity and volunteer one Saturday morning a month getting their hands dirty. I love this idea because his children are receiving a priceless education of gratitude in action. Volunteering serves multiple purposes for the family: it bonds the family together with a shared purpose and reminds them what really matters, which is loving God and loving their neighbors. Lastly, it gives your children an awareness of struggles and difficult conditions, and an appreciation for how truly blessed we are. A similar option is to sign up for an overseas mission as a family.

Correlations Between Perceptions of Parents' Generosity & Importance of Generosity

	How important is generosity to you?			
How generous were your parents?	% extremely	% very	% somewhat	% not very/ not at all
Extremely	40	11	9	3
Very	32	46	27	22
Somewhat	17	34	51	46
Not Very /not at all	11	9	12	29

For parents, teaching happens in everyday life. As your children watch you go to the bank, pay for things, or earn money, take a moment to explain what's happening and how you're dividing your earnings. They will begin to see money as a tool to be used that is never 100 percent theirs. As they grow up they will see the world as stewards, not as consumers. All of this can be done without millions in the bank— and I truly believe these are priceless lessons.

No matter your wealth level and your financial situation, you can illustrate to others how important stewardship is to your walk with Christ. Your children—and other people's children—are watching. They are listening to and watching what you are saying to make sure what they hear aligns with what they see. They will take note of your integrity. If we say that it's better to give than to receive, but we actually buy on credit and let things pile up in the garage, or if we say that we care about the poor, but most of our effort is giving to our own success at the expense of others, they will see that.

I fear if we raise our children to have a strong work ethic and to be hard-charging achievers, they will believe their idea of "making it" is the accumulation of a lot of things. You see this all the time with newlyweds who in two years are trying to have everything that their parents took thirty years to accumulate. Some younger couples want the same size house or bigger, two newer cars, all sitting on a larger lot in the same neighborhood as their parents. That might be fine, and I'm inferring a lot, but in my eyes, it raises questions, starting with: What are their values?

What I want to do is to challenge the notion that success has to do with gathering and accumulating for ourselves and even our families. When we see our lives from an eternal perspective, our wealth can do so much more.

WRITING YOUR OWN EULOGY

Writing your own eulogy can be an incredibly clarifying exercise to show you what matters to you and who gets the credit for your life. Use the prompts below to write your own eulogy and ask yourself: What does my eulogy say about me?

- What kind of person was he?
- What were some of his most notable accomplishments?
- Who is she survived by?
- Who did he most influence and how?
- What is one story about her that defines her life?

One day when I was fifteen, my mother had recently gotten off work and came through the back door. I could hear her bringing in groceries, but I started erasing and blowing off the shavings. I put my pencil back to the paper and kept writing feverishly.

She said, "Andrew can you help me with the groceries? I am going to start unpacking everything here in the kitchen."

Like many kids do, I replied, "Mom, can you give me just five minutes please?"

She said, "Sure, honey, what are you up to?"

"I am writing my eulogy," I told her.

She replied, "That's nice," but then after a brief pause, she curiously quipped, "Writing *what?*!" I repeated it. She shook her head and walked back into the kitchen.

Have you put any thought into what you want your legacy to be? What legacy you want to leave behind for your children?

When you think about what you want to leave behind when you're gone, might you consider giving away less than 100 percent of your assets to your beneficiaries? What if, instead of giving it to them, you provided a list of charities which they can choose to give to? What if you left your estate to a church or other gospel ministry?

You can give the gift of giving. You can teach the practice of stewardship. You can give your children and grandchildren the experience of giving. My hope is that they might get addicted to giving instead of becoming stuck in the cycle of spending and consuming.

The Greatest Gift

We love our families, and we want to protect them with money. American pastor and author A. W. Tozer observed:

> We are often hindered from giving up our treasures to the Lord out of fear for their safety. This is especially true when those treasures are loved by relatives and friends. But we need have no such fears. Our Lord came not to destroy but to save. Everything is safe which we commit to Him, and nothing is really safe which is not so committed.[27]

Money can be a great gift, but it can also bring on foolishness and privilege. Money is not trustworthy. Only God can protect your family.

Those who inherit wealth do not appreciate it the way that its earners did. There's no guarantee that the money will be spent wisely or in ways that will further God's kingdom. Instead, take the time now to instill in your family members the gift of generosity. Together you can join the Giving Generation. Together you can leave a lasting legacy.

Chapter 9: Reader's Guide

Biblical Text to Study: 1 Peter 1:3–5

Discussion	• How did this chapter challenge your current view on passing down wealth through generations? • What are some practical ways you can leave a legacy without leaving behind money? • Do you think you can be too transparent with your family about your finances? • Would you live life differently if you knew there was a test at the end (because there is one)?
Framework	**WRITE YOUR OWN EULOGY** If you haven't already, this can be an incredibly enlightening experience. Go back and use the framework above to write your own eulogy.
Memorization:	**1 Peter 1:3–4** *Blessed be the God and Father of our Lord Jesus Christ! According to his great mercy, he has caused us to be born again to a living hope through the resurrection of Jesus Christ from the dead, to an inheritance that is imperishable, undefiled, and unfading, kept in heaven for you.*
Group Leader Questions	• How does any treasure get hidden yet forgotten? How are we burying this gospel treasure for our children and grandchildren? • How does the parable of this Edmond Dantès like character (Count of Monte Cristo reference) convict you? Is it his joy or zeal or committedness?

CREATING AN ETERNAL INHERITANCE | 183

- In what ways does the parable challenge our priorities and evoke sacrifices we must make with our careers and relationships?
- How does the memorization scripture parallel with Proverbs 13:22?

Action item

Publish for the family an Annual Financial Report that shows where you're spending money, saving money, and giving money. Ask the family to join in to see what ideas they have to improve the balance.

Prayer

Lord, help me to live a life of urgency. Encourage me to not live slothfully. Lord, convict me when I am sitting idly by resting on your grace and refusing to work out my salvation with fear and trembling. Give me opportunities to use my talents, gifts, time, and resources to help your gospel spread. Lord, you expect a return on my life; who am I to argue? You paid the cost and you saved me, a sinner who was dead in my trespasses. Please, Holy Spirit, light a fire in me to share your gospel boldly in the byways and in the roads locally, domestically, and internationally. Amen.

CHAPTER 10

What We Lose When
We Don't Give

God made all of His creation to give.
He made the sun, the moon, the stars,
the clouds, the earth, the plants to give. He also designed
His supreme creation, man, to give. But fallen man
is the most reluctant giver in all of God's creation.
~ JOHN MCARTHUR

W e think that by controlling our money, we can control our future. Actually, the opposite is true. The harder we work to control money, the more we become controlled by our selfishness and greed.

By controlling my money, I thought I could control my future. By keeping everything close, I could better my family's position. I thought that the more I had, the better off my life would be. By getting as much as I could, by giving my time and energy over to money, I could become rich and powerful. If I managed my money well enough, if I controlled it, I would finally feel content.

Instead, I woke up from my trance one day and realized that money had its grips on me. I was worshipping money instead of my Savior. My money and my possessions dictated how I spent my time, what career choices I made, who I hung out with, and what impact I had on those around me. I gave my money and my possessions that power. I was not free to give money to important causes. My need for more dictated my decisions.

I've shared with you how I gave up every weekend to work. I was a workaholic to the extreme. I didn't go to church. I didn't spend time with anyone outside of work. Anytime people would ask me to go to something, I'd say, "Sorry, I can't." I felt compelled by my need for more. I neglected relationship after relationship, until I didn't have many friends left.

The only way out of greed is to push into generosity and let the Holy Spirit change your heart. It is safer to put this book down and say, "Well, that was nice to read about tithing. I am so glad I am already tithing." No, this book is about showing you there is a closer walk available with Christ than plainly giving 10 percent to the church. There is a better path where you don't determine how much you will give to God but how much you will keep for yourself and then give the rest back to God to utilize. The only way out of this trap is through *surrender*.

Money as a Trap

Have you ever seen a Chinese finger trap? It's a thin, flexible tube, scarcely big enough for a person to put their index fingers in either side, almost touching in the middle. It's a cheap toy, but it's amazing how effective it is: once you put both of your fingers in it, your instinct tells you to pull your fingers out quickly to free yourself.

———

The only way out of greed is to

push into generosity and let the

Holy Spirit change your heart.

———

(Squeezed)

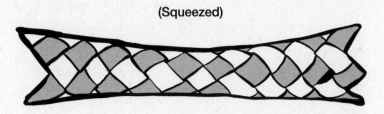

It never works because as you pull, the device contracts, squeezing your fingers even tighter. The trick is to stop pulling. When you relax and stop trying so hard, the toy loosens its grip and you can slowly extricate yourself.

When I look at the rich people around me, I so often see people with their fingers in Chinese finger traps: stuck in the rat race, stuck on the make-and-spend treadmill, owned by possessions. I don't want you to live your life that way. Is it any wonder that, according to Jesus, wealth is actually a hindrance to the kingdom of God?

In the first century, the reigning Jewish belief was that wealth and prosperity were signs of God's favor and blessings. Jesus challenged both our culture and ancient culture when He presented wealth not as a blessing or something to hold on to but as something which gets in the way. After Jesus asked the Rich Young Ruler to give up his riches and the man did not, Jesus had some commentary for His disciples:

"Truly, I say to you, only with difficulty will a rich person enter the kingdom of heaven. Again I tell you, it is easier for a camel to go through the eye of a needle than for a rich person to enter the kingdom of God." When the disciples heard this, they were greatly astonished, saying, "Who then can be saved?" (Matthew 19:23–25)

You might think that the less you have, the harder it is to give up what you have, but the opposite is true: the richer you are, the harder it becomes to let go of your wealth. The Rich Young Ruler was enslaved to his possessions, addicted to accumulation. He walked away sorrowful because he couldn't walk toward Christ and His commands. Why is it so hard for the rich to go to heaven?

Being "rich" isn't about your net worth but about your mindset. I've identified three mindsets that I believe make it challenging for the "rich" to get into the kingdom of heaven. See if any of these mindsets apply to you. How "rich" are you?

Three Attitudes Of The Rich

The rich prioritize money over God.

Instead of using their time and talent to serve God by loving people and spreading God's Word, the rich use their time and talent to accumulate more wealth for themselves.

The rich love things, not people.

God commands us to love our neighbors, to feed the poor, care for orphans, defend those who are defenseless. For those obsessed with more, getting the next thing takes priority over helping others.

The rich think they have no need of spiritual help.

Life has rewarded the rich, and it's easy for us to believe we deserve the reward or have earned it. Those who are rich do not see our need for God. Basically, money provides an opportunity for us to live for ourselves, and when given the chance to serve ourselves, so often we take it.

It's easy to think we are excused from this, because we do not see ourselves as "those rich people." If you live in America, it's highly likely that you *are* "those rich people." Again, riches are more about a mindset than about a dollar amount.

We, along with the disciples, might respond, "Who then can be saved?"

One Way out of the Trap

Fortunately, Jesus' next words answer this question: "With man this is impossible, but with God all things are possible" (Matthew 19:26). The irony is that by the world's standards, the RYR walked away with culture wiping its forehead, saying, "That was a close one." A success story by the world's standard is when the main character of the story leaves the scene riding off into the sunset with all of their money still intact. Yet we see a real-life Shakespearean tragedy ending where a Rich Young Ruler walks away poor, terminal, and impotent.

Luckily, we are not left without alternative examples. Soon after the story of the RYR, the Gospel of Luke presents the story of Zacchaeus.

Zacchaeus' interaction with Jesus and the Rich Young Ruler's situation have some striking parallels. While Zacchaeus is not a ruler, he is named as a tax collector—a man with relative wealth in the community. While we do not know how the RYR acquired wealth, tax collectors were known for cheating those around them, inflating taxes in order to take a larger percentage for themselves. As a chief tax collector, he was shut out from communing with his community and even shut out from seeing Jesus without climbing a tree. Today, we vote for laws on state and federal taxes, but back in Roman times, they farmed out taxes to the highest bidder. It was like a public auction to raise taxes in certain areas. Every time Zacchaeus collected his fellow Jews' taxes, he was in essence making them bow to Caesar. Zacchaeus and the Rich Young Ruler had different backgrounds, but both were eager to meet Jesus and seek Him out.

In each case, Jesus saw right to the man's heart. In the RYR's case, he walks away sad. Zacchaeus' response to Jesus is dramatically different:

> And when Jesus came to the place, he looked up and said to him, "Zacchaeus, hurry and come down, for I must stay at your house today." So he hurried and came down and received him joyfully. And when they saw it, they all grumbled, "He has gone in to be the guest of a man who is a sinner." And Zacchaeus stood and said to the Lord, "Behold, Lord, the half of my goods I give to the poor. And if I have defrauded anyone of anything, I restore it fourfold." And Jesus said to him, "Today salvation has come to this house, since he also is a son of Abraham. For the Son of Man came to seek and to save the lost" (Luke 19:5–10).

Zacchaeus welcomed Jesus into his home and immediately gave abundantly to the poor. He gave his wealth away. This is the appropriate response: it demonstrates repentance, gratitude, and a fresh caring for community. It's the natural reaction toward salvation. Gratitude fills the new Christian and generosity flows out. It's as if you breathe in gratitude and you breathe out generosity. Loosening our grip on what we think is "ours" brings us the meaning we were looking for in the first place. D. L. Moody once said, "For when men begin to make restitution, the world will have confidence in the religion we preach."[28]

Freedom at Last

"Pushing your finger" in or "coming down" means you must decide. It is hard to surrender. Coming down is humbling—it's admitting you're a sinner in need of saving. I remember my walk down the aisle at age eleven; it's a humbling feeling to climb out of the pew and walk toward Jesus. Now, you may say, "I have already done that." If so, then, my brother or sister, let me challenge your spiritual maturity. Are you still as grateful as you were on the day of your salvation? Do you remember when Jesus looked at you and even, despite your sin, called you by name? When I think about that moment for me, my response beckons, "Jesus, take 10 percent; better yet, take it all," because I now have what I was seeking all along.

Our response should be like Zacchaeus:

+ Who can I help introduce Jesus to? – *Stay at my house.*
+ How can I support the gospel to go out where it hasn't been preached? – *Half my goods I give to the poor.*
+ What ministry do I need to get involved with physically and financially? – *And if I have defrauded anyone of anything, I restore it fourfold.*

Make haste, come down from that tree. Jesus is asking you to decide. You don't have eternity but merely a lifetime (shorter than we think) to choose and respond to salvation. As Charles Spurgeon said, "The road to perdition is laid all over with branches of trees whereon men are sitting, for they often pull down branches from the trees but they do not come down themselves."[29]

Will you walk away, or will you come down? How will you respond?

Chapter 10: Reader's Guide

Biblical Text to Study Luke 19:1–10

Discussion	• Do you think the zealousness of Zacchaeus should be confined to salvation? • Why do you think the Bible mentions his size? We know his identity changed. Similar to the Grinch, I believe his heart grew three sizes. • Don't procrastinate. Remember to make haste; as Charles Spurgeon said, "The road to perdition is laid all over with branches of trees whereon men are sitting, for they often pull down branches from the trees but they do not come down themselves."
Framework	**The Chinese Finger Trap** It's harder than a camel to go through the eye of a needle and harder to pull yourself out of a Chinese finger trap. What areas of your financial affairs do you need to release to the Lord?
Memorization	**Luke 19:8** *But Zacchaeus stood up and said to the Lord, "Look, Lord! Here and now I give half of my possessions to the poor, and if I have cheated anybody out of anything, I will pay back four times the amount"* (NIV).
Group Leader Questions	• How do D. L. Moody's words come to life after reading about Zacchaeus' transformation? "For when men begin to make restitution, the world will have confidence in the religion we preach." • What parallels can you draw from the narrator of *A Christmas Carol* described by Ebeneezer Scrooge as, "'Oh! but he

was a tight-fisted hand at the grindstone, Scrooge! A squeezing, wrenching, grasping, scraping, clutching, covetous old sinner!'"

- Why do you think Zacchaeus was so interested in seeing Jesus? Was he interested in getting in on the ground floor like his tax franchise he had secured from the Roman Empire?
- Did you catch Jesus calling out to Zacchaeus without knowing his name?
- Is it possible that our stinginess comes from forgetting that we, too, once fell out of a tree into grace? Have we forgotten walking down an aisle toward our Savior?

Action Item	**Take the Giver's Pledge:** I, _____, won't wait to give my resources until I have passed and I no longer need them. Instead, I will sacrifice now. I will set income limits and think differently about generational wealth and make it my mission to inspire a movement of Christians called the Giving Generation.
Prayer	Lord, I confess that I've lost too much time in my unwillingness to be generous with you and your church. Thank you for guiding me on this journey and for showing me how I was trapped. I pray that in your wisdom you would invite me even further into generosity. Make me a disciple so that I can make others a disciple for you. Amen.

Gratitude Fuels Generosity

*As base a thing as money often is, yet it can be
transmuted into everlasting treasure. It can be converted
into food for the hungry and clothing for the poor. It
can keep a missionary actively winning lost men to
the light of the gospel and thus transmute itself into
heavenly values. Any temporal possession can be
turned into everlasting wealth. Whatever is given to
Christ is immediately touched with immortality.*

~ W. TOZER

Your paycheck may say your name, but the truth is, it's not your money. You may feel like you've worked really hard to get where you are, and you could probably even list the hours you've logged, the degrees you've earned, and the times you've gone above and beyond to achieve the position you've found. The truth is, none of it belongs to you, not your talents, not your treasure, and certainly not your money.

When you really start to let this sink in, you no longer have to coerce yourself to give. When you see how much you have been given (and *forgiven*), generosity becomes second nature.

Your paycheck may say your name, but the truth is, it's not your money.

In fact, your generosity is a reflection of your gratitude. The more grateful you are, the more generous you will be. This is not purely an opinion I have. It's a law of nature. Gratitude is what you breathe in, generosity is what you breathe out. As you reflect on your generosity in the next exercise, I want you to ask yourself what your generosity says about your gratitude.

Maybe you don't need to force yourself to be more generous. Maybe you need to spend more time reflecting on what you've been *given*.

God is very clear that there will be a judgment for believers and that we should live our lives in a way that will make our Creator and Father proud. If as you reflect you realize that aren't proud of the way you are living, maybe it's time to ask yourself: Am I grateful enough for what I've been given? And if not, how can I cultivate more gratitude?

Your gratitude *fuels* your generosity.

Become an Everyday Philanthropist

When we begin to experience a sense of gratitude for all that has been given to us, we naturally become what I call Everyday Philanthropists.

Contrary to popular belief, philanthropists are not just old dudes who drive nice cars and attend fancy galas. Philanthropists are people, regular people, who *give* generously of their resources. They give away a large percentage of their income and assets.

————

Gratitude is what you

breathe in, generosity is

what you breathe out.

————

EXIT INTERVIEW

All of our lives are coming to an end, just like a job or career that we know won't last. You can think of this life as a temporary assignment or a summer job. During this "internship" (life) you have been hired, observed, and given perks unique to you. You were given all of the blessings you have lived with all of these years, and one day you and I will have to give an orderly account.

No thought is more sobering for a believer and nonbeliever than the thought of standing face-to-face with the Creator of the universe, sitting there in all of His glory and honor upon His seat of judgment.

My salvation is intact and no one can pluck me from His hand. However, it concerns me how many times over my life I have willingly chosen my own direction instead of yielding my life and blessings to God. Remember, God knows every single hair on my head and every single motive I have ever had, along with all the sins and buried thoughts I am not proud of.

We will never know until we are face-to-face with Jesus what exactly He will ask of us. However, the following are some questions He might ask of each of us when that day comes.

When He comes for all of us, or if He comes individually for you, may our Master find us busy at work.

Here are some of those possible questions to reflect on:

- How did you help the least of these? Specifically, orphans, widows, captives, the poor, sojourners, and the downcast?

- How did you leverage the abilities I designed in you?
- Who did you have intentional talks with about the good news that you received?
- Have you read my handbook (the Bible)?
- Who did you forgive with my strength helping you?
- Who did you forgive that was unforgivable?
- How did you utilize the salary, fringe benefits, bonuses, and other income I heaped upon your life?
- Have you spoken to your colleagues? Did you pray for them often?
- Who did you train and disciple?
- Who did you support and be vulnerable enough with to let them know they weren't alone?
- What did you sacrifice for my name?
- If I have an open door policy, then how much time weekly did you spend with me?
- Tell me where and how you served and promoted the kingdom to come.

I assure you, the exit interview with Christ at the end of the age will be thorough. He will have plenty of time to do it, and He will command our attention unlike any boss we have ever had. He will cover all of our wrongdoings and the times we helped the least of these. He will ask about our biblical stewardship. He will take us through our lives like a Netflix show, skipping commercials and pauses and replaying all the times we were given raises, promotions, windfalls, inheritances and—instead of choosing to use it for the betterment of the holy universal church and the furthering of the gospel—we chose our own wants and desires.

> Will we try to justify our actions to Christ, saying, "But God, you have to understand, the cultural pressure of the day was to make all that I could and spend what I didn't need for a later!" To no one's surprise, that mindset won't pass the test. We have to make a choice today, challenged by the Holy Spirit, to say, "I am walking away from the world's agenda for my finances. I will no longer consume everything I have. I will no longer continue to store up treasures here on earth."
>
> Earthly treasures will never make you complete.

Percentage says nothing about how much you make. There's no bar. By this definition, a child could be a philanthropist. You can be a philanthropist at sixteen with your first job. You can be a philanthropist now.

Everyday philanthropy is the result of a heart that is surrendered to God's will. It is the outcome of obedience and trust. Take a minute to use the Everyday Philanthropy Assessment and see how you score.

God Is Searching for Stewards

As you give, you will also find that God trusts you with more (Matthew 25:23). The Lord is looking for great stewards to trust. Look at Joseph, whose journey of stewardship was full of trials, yet he was blessed for his enduring trust in God. Look at a modern-day steward like Truett Cathy, founder of Chick-fil-A. In 1982 Chick-fil-A faced a crisis as competition from other fast-food chains caused its revenues to fall.

Truett Cathy and company executives retreated to a resort at Georgia's Lake Lanier to find an answer to their problem. That group of executives pondered the question, "Why are we in business?" Cathy said they came up with a corporate statement: "To glorify God by being

THE EVERYDAY PHILANTHROPY QUIZ

For each item below, rate yourself on a scale of 0 to 3.

0: This doesn't sound like me at all.

1: This sounds like me every now and then.

2: This describes me most of the time, but not all.

3: This describes me nearly all of the time.

1. I'm quick to give.
2. When I see a need in the church, I automatically extend help.
3. I consistently put a percentage of my income aside to give.
4. I plan to give; it's a regular part of my finances.
5. I model generosity for my children. It's a value I plan to pass on.
6. Being generous brings me joy.
7. I'm excited to give and look for opportunities to do so.
8. As my income increases, my giving is exponentially growing.
9. I give of my time, energy, and skills toward the kingdom.
10. I volunteer. I listen to people. I learn from others.

Add up your number and . . .

If you scored 0 to 10:

Thankfully, God is a God of grace, and He gives us endless chances to grow closer to Him. Knowing where you have work to do is more than half the battle.

If you scored 11 to 20:

Falling in the middle might make you feel like you're "doing okay" as it relates to giving. But what if God wants to use you to do more? Where are you falling short? Where is the Holy Spirit inviting you to go further?

If you scored 21 to 30:

You are a true Everyday Philanthropist. Your call, now, is to inspire those around you. Who can you invite into generosity with you? How can you teach your church, your family, or your community the way of Everyday Philanthropy that you've learned?

a faithful steward of all that is entrusted to us, and to have a positive influence on all who come in contact with Chick-fil-A."

In six months, sales increased 40 percent. Cathy was not only well-known for being the founder of Chick-fil-A but also for his faith in Jesus Christ. He is also known for taking a stand to close his restaurants on Sundays (even though it costs him millions of dollars), for being a Sunday school teacher, and for helping many foster children. Chick-fil-A is the largest private, family-owned restaurant chain in America. What a legacy.

Everyday philanthropy can change the lives of the people you give to, but it also can change your own life .

Find the Sweetness of Life

When we become aware of the needs of other people, it helps us have perspective on our own difficulties as well. I believe when you begin to give aid to those who are less fortunate and who can never repay you, it shifts the focus away from yourself and onto how you can help others, invigorating you with a newfound passion and purpose.

You will find yourself with a changed heart. You will care more for the poor. You will become more grateful. Your spiritual life will change. I've become convinced that giving money away is the best thing I can do for my soul: it keeps me humble, and it keeps me looking to and depending on God. If you can trust in the process of consistent giving of your time, resources, and talents into something larger than yourself, I know the Lord will give you deep joy.

The more you give, the sweeter your life becomes. You can't outgive God. Malachi 3:10 says, "'Bring the whole tithe into the storehouse, that there may be food in my house. Test me in this,' says the LORD Almighty, 'and see if I will not throw open the floodgates of heaven and pour out so much blessing that there will not be room enough to store it'" (NIV). In Luke 6:38, Jesus said, "Give, and it will be given to you. Good measure, pressed down, shaken together, running over, will be put into your lap. For with the measure you use it will be measured back to you."

You can't outgive God.

God's blessings keep coming.

I've seen this in my own life as well. God doesn't only give back to me in financial abundance and security. He also gives back to me in gratitude, in peace, in the ability to step off that treadmill, in purpose and meaning. We might not always get our rewards on this side of paradise, but they will come. In the meantime, I'm living a fuller, more peaceful life.

Build a Lasting Legacy

Can you tell me the names of your great-grandparents? Can you tell me their parents' names? In my experience, few of us remember even the names of our family members only a few generations back. I call this the great-grandparent test. It reveals how quickly our legacies fade.

What we *do* remember are movements of faithful people who changed the course of history forever.

The hard truth is that even the Rich Young Rulers will be shortly forgotten. Even the wealthiest and most influential of us have legacies which do not last. It doesn't matter if you are Mark Zuckerberg or Joe from down the street; life, at its longest, is short.

James 4:14 says, "Yet you do not know what tomorrow will bring. What is your life? For you are a mist that appears for a little time and then vanishes." Your greatest chance at making an impact is to band together with other believers in a new generation of generosity: the Giving Generation.

By yourself, you're unlikely to make an impact that lasts—despite how much you desire to. You're more likely to get trapped by your wealth, lost in the hustle, or easily forgotten (even by your family) a few years after you're gone. When you come together with your spouse, your family, your children, your grandchildren, your community, and even the global church—when you join the Giving Generation—you can help change the course of history forever.

After the Rich Young Ruler left in sadness, Jesus' conversation in Matthew 19 continued. Jesus said to His disciples, "Everyone who has left houses or brothers or sisters or father or mother or children or lands, for my name's sake, will receive a hundredfold and will inherit eternal life. But many who are first will be last, and the last first" (Matthew 19:29–30). You might not be rich in this world's sense of rich, but you will be rich toward God. You will have everlasting treasure. You will have God's love, peace, mercy, and joy.

This is the kind of treasure which we can take with us when we die. It's also the kind of treasure which makes a lasting impression on those who we leave behind.

Whether you're struggling in your finances, well-established and thriving, or retired, you have a choice about the legacy you want to leave behind you: Do you want your legacy to last?

Choose to give to gospel ministries. Choose to spread the good news. Choose to help the poor. Choose to take care of the sick. Choose to love your neighbor. There are people out there who need to know that God loves them.

One of the best ways to bring meaning to your own life and make a lasting, eternal difference in the lives of so many others is to give. It's to tithe to your local church and reach people in your community. It's to give to missionaries who are intentionally sharing God's love. It's to provide practical help—food, water, clothing, shelter, medical attention—to those in need. It is to care for widows and orphans (James 1:27). Our goal can no longer be to leave a lasting inheritance in an attempt to prolong the heritage of our last name. It is to continue the work of one name alone: Jesus.

After a hundred years pass, your last name may cease to exist, but one name will remain. Your giving can be a part of this legacy of spreading the good news that will outlast every family tree. Your children's children's children may not know your name, but what is of God lasts forever.

The Giving Generation has the opportunity to see the 3 *billion* people who have no access to God finally hear the name of Jesus Christ in their language. The Giving Generation could be the generation that see's Christ's return, not only because of the culmination of the signs of the end of the age (Matthew 24:3–8). No, the Giving Generation could see Christ's return because finally all the world has been reached by the news of the gospel (Matthew 24:14). I believe this future can become a reality in our lifetime if you and I begin to give radically.

Become the Giving Generation

Being rich, young, and powerful by the world's standards will always disappoint. If you want to be rich, be rich toward God: be rich in generosity and in sacrifice for others (Luke 12:21). If you want to stay young, then you must become a new creation, letting go of your old self (the one on the make-and-spend treadmill) and becoming a person of generosity (2 Corinthians 5:17). Lastly, if you seek power and want to be great, you will find these things through the Spirit at work within as you help the least of those among you. You will find greatness as you serve the poor, orphaned, widowed, displaced, imprisoned, and lost (Ephesians 3:20 and Matthew 23:11).

I used to hear that voice in my head, tearing me down no matter how much I had accomplished, telling me, "You can do better. You think you've made it? You're not doing nearly enough. You can make more, have more, be more." I don't hear that voice nearly as often now. Instead, I know that God through me is making an impact for the kingdom, and I know my life has eternal meaning. Instead, I hear the words of Jesus through Paul: "It is more blessed to give than to receive" (Acts 20:35).

As you read this, I'm praying those words over you. I pray you find the freedom and hope I've found in everyday giving. I pray you join me for a life of meaning and joy as part of the Giving Generation.

Chapter 11: Reader's Guide

Biblical Text to Study: 1 Timothy 6:17–19

Discussion

- As for the age we live in today what does it look like to be self-sufficient in our own lives? Can an a emergency fund coupled with a solid career, large 401k balance, and a paid off home lead us to be arrogant?
- How practically can you and I create more margin in our finances to give at a moments notice when the spirit leads?
- Do you spend enough time thinking about the treasure you are sending ahead into the next kingdom? How does thinking about God preparing a place for you right now encourage you in packing the "moving truck" in this life?
- How can we put the instruction to do "good works" into practice?
- Have you stolen God's glory lately? This week, how can you boast publicly in Christ instead of your riches?

Framework

Exit Interview

If you haven't yet, go back to the exit interview from this chapter and answer the questions quietly to yourself. Let God convict your heart.

Memorization

1 Timothy 6:17 *Command those who are rich in this present age not to be haughty, nor to trust in uncertain riches but in the living God, who gives us richly all things to enjoy* (NKJV).

Group Leader Questions

- The wealthy were to be coddled and waited upon instead of being charged with a responsibility to give. Look at how this verse parallels James 2:1–13, which talks about the common practice of showing favoritism. Do you think we still do this today?
- How can riches disillusion us to believe they are reliable and trustworthy?
- How can we create an environment in our home to foster giving instead of focusing merely on making and spending?
- What ways can you teach your children and grandchildren about how money works and how they can become better stewards of what they have been given?
- How does 1 Timothy 6:17–19 parallel Psalm 49:11–12?

Action Item

Write out your giving vision. Discuss and commit as a family what your limit to fulfillment will be. Write a financial mission statement for the family. Discuss together the impact this increased giving will have on your local church and the ministries your family feels passionately about. Involve the whole family in this process as you discuss its future effects on their individual walks with Christ and how living with an open heart and open hand can have an everlasting impact for the gospel. Commit the whole family to this action and have them all pitch in and take an individual stake. Update all family members as you give toward these important ministries. For example, our financial mission statement is, "The McNair family will strive to give 50 percent or more of our income away toward furthering the gospel; we will wisely invest 30 percent and maintain a standard of living of 20 percent or less."

Prayer   Lord, you have instructed us to be radically generous of all the blessings you have endowed us with. Help us to put our hope in you alone. Turn our eyes from idols, possessions, and pursuits of this world, and raise our gaze toward heaven. Guide us in discipling others in biblical stewardship, and create a legacy of meeting the needs of those around us and giving sacrificially to spread the gospel. In Jesus' name, amen.

Bonus Action   Now that you are allowing God to transform your approach to money, share the love. **Ask your pastor or home group about reading this book together.**

Notes

Introduction

1   Barna Group, *The State of Generosity*, (Ventura, CA, 2021), https://www.barna.com/state-of-generosity/.

2   John Ronsvalle and Sylvia Ronsvalle, *The State of Church Giving through 2019: Serve God with Money At-Scale or Serve Money*, (Eugene, OR: Wipf and Stock Publishers, 2022).

3   "21 Fascinating Tithing Statistics," Health Research Funding, https://healthresearchfunding.org/21-tithing-statistics/.

4   C. J. Maheney, *Worldliness: Resisting the Seduction of a Fallen World* (Wheaton, IL: Crossway, 2008), 23.

5   See C. S. Lewis, *Mere Christianity* (London, England: Geoffrey Bles , 1952).

6   Matt. 10:34

7   Rev. 3:14–22

8   Brandon Park, "2,350 Bible Verses on Money," November 30, 2017, https://churchleaders.com/outreach-missions/outreach-missions-articles/314227-2350-bible-verses-money.html.

9   Sheryl Nance-Nash, "Is The Bible The Ultimate Financial Guide?" Forbes, https://www.forbes.com/sites/sherylnancenash/2012/05/24/is-the-bible-the-ultimate-financial-guide/?sh=5affc95e6493.

10 Heb. 7:1–3.

11 Gen. 28:10–22.

12 Ps. 50.

Chapter 1

13 Carl Yung, *The Collected Works of C. G. Jung, Volume 16: Practice of Psychotherapy*, 2nd ed. (New Jersey: Princeton University Press, 2014).

14 Andrew Carnegie, *The Gospel of Wealth and Other Timely Essays*, (Cambridge, MA: Harvard University Press, 1962)

Chapter 3

15 John Piper, *Don't Waste Your Life*, (Wheaton, IL: Crossway, 2018).

Chapter 4

16 See The Spending Pyramid from Chapter 3.

17 Learn more about Jim Rohn at www.jimrohn.com/.

Chapter 5

18 "9 World Poverty Statistics that Everyone Should Know," LifeWater, January 28, 2020, https://lifewater.org/blog/9-world-poverty-statistics-to-know-to-day/.

19 Ashlea Ebeling, "Average Tax Refund Up 11% in 2021," *Forbes*, November 1, 2021. https://www.forbes.com/sites/ashleaebeling/2021/11/01/tax-re-funds-up-11-in-2021/?sh=226a205a7739.

20 Consult a CPA if you have questions about your tax withholding.

Chapter 6

21 Francis Chan, "Pastor Francis Chan on his downsized lifestyle," interview by Mike Huckabee, *Huckabee*, Fox News, February 3, 2017.

22 Stanley T. Ling, adaptation of Charles Edward White, "What Did Wesley Practice and Preach About Money," West Ohio Conference, The United Methodist Church, December 2019. https://www.westohioumc.org/confer-ence/news/what-did-wesley-practice-and-preach-about-money.

23 Mike Holmes, "What Would Happen if the Church Tithed?" *Relevant*, updated June 15, 2021, https://relevantmagazine.com/faith/church/what-would-happen-if-church-tithed/.

Chapter 7

24 Jacqueline E. Lapsley, Carol A. Newsom, Sharon H. Ringe, , *Women's Bible Commentary*, 3rd ed. (Louisville, KY: Westminster John Knox Press, 2012), 353.

25 Example from a sermon by David Platt, Lead Pastor, McLean Bible Church, Vienna, VA.

Chapter 9

26 Carnegie, *The Gospel of Wealth*.

27 A. W. Tozer, *The Pursuit of God* (Abbotsford, WI: Aneko Press, 2015).

Chapter 10

28 Dwight L. Moody, W. H. Daniels, *Moody: His Words, Work, and Workers* (New York: Nelson & Phillips, 1877), 248.

29 C. H. Spurgeon, "Effectual Calling," (sermon, New Park Street Chapel, Southwark, London, March 30, 1856), https://www.spurgeon.org/resource-library/sermons/effectual-calling/#flipbook/.